CHEERS TO YOUR
FREEDOM !

Michelle

DON'T BE "THAT GUY" IN NETWORK MARKETING

DON'T BE "THAT GUY" IN NETWORK MARKETING

Adam & Michelle Carey

NEXT CENTURY
PUBLISHING

Don't Be "That Guy" in Network Marketing
Copyright ©2015 by Adam & Michelle Carey

Published by Next Century Publishing
Las Vegas, Nevada
www.NextCenturyPublishing.com

ISBN: 978-1-68102-091-4

Printed in the United States of America

Illustrations are the creation of Travis Nix
www.travisnixart.com

For more information, please visit: AdamAndMichelleCarey.com

"That Guy" –Urban Dictionary

noun

The person everyone loves to hate and never wants to become. *Making these 21 common mistakes will cause people to label you as "That Guy."*

Table of Contents

Introduction.. 13

Acknowledgements.. 17

"That Guy" in Network Marketing 21

The Sneak-Attack MLMer 27

The Secret Agent 33

The Lack Listener 39

The Motor Mouth 43

The Social Media Spammer.. 49

The "Oh, by the Way" Phone Caller 55

The Long-Winded Writer 59

The Bait and Slammer 63

Negative Nancy and Poor-Me Paul 69

The Nose Deaf and Disheveled..................................... 77

The Defensive Tackler 85

The Stalker 89

The Con-Vincer 97

The Snake Oil Salesman 103

The Know-It-All.. 107

The Haughty on a High Horse 113

The Basher 119

The Time Stealer 125

The Prospect Thief 131

The MLM Junkie 137

The Networking Group Tasmanian Devil 145

Conclusion.. 149

Notes 151

DON'T BE "THAT GUY" IN NETWORK MARKETING

Introduction

We love network marketing. This profession has truly changed our lives. However, it wasn't always rainbows and unicorns; we had to weather many storms, especially in the initial seasons of our business. When we were introduced to network marketing, we didn't have any business or leadership experience. We always joke with our mentor that we were a huge project, and we thank her and all the other people who poured so much of their wisdom into us. With their help along with God's blessings and provision, we were able to make our dreams come true in this profession.

We decided to write this book because we see a disconnect between the reality of network marketing and the way much of society views it. Many people believe network marketing is beneath them, but from our perspective, everything they want—uncapped income, leverage, time freedom, and little financial risk—is available as a package only in network marketing.

Network marketing professionals, or should we say *unprofessionals*, are the reason behind this negative perspective. We include ourselves in this category because we have made these mistakes and have been "That Guy" many times. Really, we're not all bad people who lay our heads on our pillows at night with a maniacal laugh and scheme up ways to burn our friends.

Network marketing professionals are good people who make mistakes because we simply don't know *not* to make them. These mistakes may have been modeled by certain leaders and were then passed down through their teams like a bad generational iniquity. And again, we've done the same, so please don't think we're standing on a podium pointing fingers at everyone else. You will see throughout this book that in the majority of these mistakes, we are pointing the finger at ourselves!

Also, the mistakes we discuss may seem like common sense, but they're not. If they were, so many people out there wouldn't be making them over and over again. That's what makes these mistakes so deadly: people don't think they need to watch out for them! They're like an insidious virus infecting the organization and crippling it from reaching its potential.

We want this book to be entertaining, and we want this book to be value-packed with tips that can truly transform your business and your team. At times, we may get passionate and you may feel a little butt kicking, but just know that we are writing it out of love. We've been there, and we'd rather you not go down the same path.

If you want your team to flourish but dread the awkward conversation about how they're unknowingly acting like "That Guy," we recommend taking a preemptive strike and getting this book into the hands of all your leaders, business partners, and every new person who joins your team. Let us have the awkward conversation for you, especially with those who have already been in the business. They may read these chapters and be able to see that they're making some of these mistakes. And here's the best news of all: they can do it privately and begin to make changes instantly without you having to intervene.

We are a husband-and-wife team, and we both passionately poured our experiences into this book. This is how the book will read: Michelle, who for some reason made more of these mistakes, writes a lot of the stories and examples of "That Guy." Adam, who is a master at coaching, provides the tips to implement in your business. We have equal parts in our contributions; Michelle loves telling stories and Adam thrives on giving meaty take-aways. We hope you enjoy reading this book—and that it transforms the way that people on your team represent network marketing.

Acknowledgements

We would like to thank all the people who were victims of these mistakes, for allowing us to bait and slam you or flood your Facebook feed with annoying posts. If it weren't for your rejection, we would have never been able to write the material for *Don't Be "That Guy" in Network Marketing*.

By now, you should know that we rarely take ourselves seriously. However, we would like to take a moment and thank some people we love.

First and foremost, we would love to thank our Lord and Savior, Jesus. Thank you for your provision and relationship. So many times we prayed and you answered our prayers. Through our experiences in the "wilderness," you instilled character in us. We were able to have encounters with you that will forever mark us, and we excitedly await more encounters with your amazing love. You are our guiding light and the foundation on which everything is built. We thank you and we love you, Father God.

We would like to thank our parents for always being supportive. To "Yoyo" and "Yoya" for always being willing to watch Hannah. There are so many times when you save us by watching her while we take an important phone call or by traveling with us so we can attend a conference while you spend hours and hours with her in the hotel room! We could not have done this without your support, and we are forever thankful.

In all honesty, we could write a separate book only about everything you have done for us.

Brother Mike, your comedic perspective even through life's challenges is an inspiration to both of us. We have shared an endless amount of inside jokes. My love for humor began with you. I have always looked up to you. Thank you for being an amazing big brother.

To my father, Chris, you have always been my biggest cheerleader, supporter, and closest friend. Thank you for always believing and encouraging me throughout the years! Tiffany, thank you for all your love and support! You have such a giving heart, and we admire your desire to serve and contribute to others. We are blessed to have you in our family!

Mom (Cheryl), thank you for always expressing your love to me; I will always be your little boy. I've always wanted to make you proud, and it means the world that you let me know that I have, time and time again.

Grandma Char and Grandpa Ralph, you both have had such a huge impact on my life and I'm so grateful for all the memories we have shared. Grandpa, I wish you could have met Hannah before heading to heaven. Grandma, thank you for your constant love and encouragement as our young family enjoys this wild ride called life!

Uncle Jeff Rosellini, you are one of the most generous, kind, and caring people I know. You have blessed Michelle, Hannah, and I more than you will ever know. Thank you for believing in us!

Grandma Pat and Grandpa George, you guys have been there with us every step of the way during our entrepreneurial journey! Thank you for always extending love and hospitality by opening your home to our team as they travel through town. Grandma, I will forever cherish our deep conversations about Jesus and the amazing life we get to experience.

Mark, you have done so much for me ever since I was a child. Thank you for helping light my entrepreneurial spark. Your love and support has meant so much to me.

Amy Harbour and Lisa Badgley, I'm so thankful that our blended families brought me two incredible big sisters. I have never considered you "step" anything, I love you both so much and have learned a great deal from watching you pursue big goals and dreams. Your families are precious and I value each time we get to come together and create new memories.

Jimmy and Gina Moore, you guys are amazing! Jimmy you have been the most incredible, dependable, and generous friend I've ever had. I still remember us sitting at The Habit Burger in Roseville, California when I mentioned Michelle and I were considering network marketing. I have to admit your enthusiasm for the industry helped me jump in with both feet! Gina you are an incredible woman and so loved by our family (Jimmy too). Thank you both for always supporting our family and business, and thank you for cat sitting every time we travel. Our cats love you too.

Esther Spina, thank you for being our business and spiritual mentor. The day you pulled us aside and took us under your wing forever changed our lives. Thank you for the many heart-to-heart talks. The season that we worked in your office taught us more about business than any college courses we have taken. Also, thank you, Frank, for always being so hospitable and for adopting us and allowing us to raid your fridge during the many times we basically lived at your house.

Brian McClure, thank you for your training center and for allowing us to learn from you and other top leaders every Saturday morning for an entire year. Thank you for believing in us so much that you allowed us to start training at your center. It was at your training center that our love for training and speaking was birthed in our hearts.

To our company leadership who poured into us, thank you! Mary and Richard Amoedo, we appreciate all the heart-to-heart talks and all the wisdom that you continue to pour into us. When we first showed up, we felt like little kids. Through your guidance in our personal development, we gained the knowledge and confidence to become professionals. Thank you, Tina Henderson, for always believing in us. You have such a generous heart.

Team Legacy, thank you for your hard work and dedication. We are honored to work along side you to achieve your dreams.

And to all the people who have been praying for us (there are too many to list), we thank you because we know that through your prayers, we were able to get this far.

"That Guy" in Network Marketing

Have you ever had a run-in with "That Guy"? He's the one who makes everyone shudder when they see his number pop up on their caller ID. She's the one who gets "un-friended" and "un-followed" on social media platforms. He's the one who finds himself in the "NFL"—the "No Friends Left" club. Unfortunately, there's a whole tribe of people who have joined the "No Friends Left" club, and if you can't think of anyone, well then "That Guy" maybe you!

That was a joke, but these constantly-made mistakes are not a laughing matter. People don't end up in the "NFL" just because they joined network marketing. They end up in the "NFL" because they make common mistakes that many network marketers make. I must admit that I have made many of these mistakes. Both Adam and I have been "That Guy."

When we learned how to conduct our network marketing business properly, our results drastically improved. We have been in the trenches of network marketing, fighting for freedom with the many families we work with. Over the years we have seen so many of these blunders trip up hard-working hopefuls. I guess that's why we're so passionate about getting this information out there!

Our profession is, for lack of a better term, frowned upon by some of our society. *How can this be?* You may be thinking. *Network marketing is amazing! You can start an already-proven franchise-like system with little investment and earn enough residual income to walk away from your job or traditional headache-ridden business to have complete ownership of your time.*

That does sound amazing. So why is it that when you mention you're in network marketing, you run the risk of people looking at you like you just told them you're an axe murderer? Again, it's because people who are untrained or not trained properly are out there making mistakes. Their friends and families end up with a bad taste in their mouth, and the next time another network marketing business is mentioned, walls come up and ears are closed to a potentially life-changing opportunity.

As Kevin O'Leary from *Shark Tank* would say, "Stop the madness!" It's time to represent our amazing profession…well, *professionally!* Let's spread the word and make people aware of the mistakes so these gaffs can be avoided. Together, we can change society's view of network marketing so people can truly see it for what it is.

We are at the dawn of an age where network marketing will be the norm. I truly, without a shadow of a doubt, believe that. All signs of our changing economy point to it. If you don't believe me, take a look at Eric Worre's documentary, *Rise of the Entrepreneur,* and you'll agree that you've made the right decision by starting a network marketing business.

Adam and I are so proud of you for moving outside the box. The best rewards in life often come when we step out and do something different. While many people may not like or understand network marketing, there are scores of people who are unhappy, broke, and starved for time, and that may be the very clue to indicate that a different path must be taken.

Make this the moment you draw a line in the sand and stake your claim that you're going to give your family the time freedom and memories you all deserve. Let's work together to make sure you perform effectively and professionally.

There's so much that Adam and I want to share with you. This is a great place to start. Here are 21 mistakes to avoid so you don't get labeled as "That Guy." Cheers to you as you embark on your journey toward massive success!

It's Nice to Meet You

I know we're all pressed for time and you want to get right to the meat of this book, but I want to share our story with you because I think it's important for you to know who you're learning from. Feel free to skip this part if you're ready for the meat. It won't hurt our feelings—and don't worry, I'm not going to spout off our income, describe the exotic vacations we take, or talk about the promotion levels we've achieved or any stats like that. Why? Because that doesn't matter. What matters is the information that will help you and your team, but if you'd like to get acquainted with us, then read on.

Adam and I were introduced to network marketing in our early twenties. Adam was in luxury boat sales and I was a retail manager at a mall, which is the worst possible place for a shopaholic (actually, former shopaholic) to work. I racked up seven credit cards just while shopping on my lunch breaks.

In 2008, the housing market started to really suffer here in California. A record number of people foreclosed on their homes, and as a result, Adam was out of work almost overnight. We were introduced to the company we currently work with and struggled to get the business off the ground. Even though we were able to make several hundred dollars a month (our goal in the beginning), we were desperate for a more stable and substantial income.

After the housing crash, we ended up with jobs waiting tables and parking cars. Not that there's anything wrong with those jobs, but they were the toughest jobs we've ever had. (So please, when you go out to a restaurant or park your car with a valet attendant, be kind and generous to them. Their jobs are not easy.)

Anyway, we were struggling because we were doing everything wrong! If you've worried that you looked like a poser by making some mistakes, let this encourage you: we've made these mistakes too. The good news is, we became students of true professionals in network marketing and other subjects, and their instruction made us more effective in our network marketing business. We are still students, which means we can keep you up to date with fresh content to learn from (for free weekly training content, visit AdamandMichelleCarey.com).

Long story short, we are now both stay-at-home parents. We love having ownership of our time, because ownership allows us to delegate that time to what is most important to us: God, creating memories with our family, and helping others achieve time ownership and freedom. We believe that if families had more time freedom and less worry about finances, our world picture would be radically different.

What if people didn't have to sit in traffic on their morning and evening commutes? Or if they didn't have debt collectors blowing up their phones every day? Or if they didn't have to wonder if their business would stay afloat because they haven't made profit on their one-time investment of several thousand dollars? Imagine if people didn't have to shove their lunch down their throat to get back to the office in time. I'd say, "What a wonderful world!"

Somehow, work has become a priority over family time in our society. Adam and I believe in working hard, but we believe more strongly in having the right lineup of priorities. That's our passion, and if that fires you up, then you're in the right place!

So, back to the 21 mistakes to avoid so you don't get labeled as "That Guy."

1

The Sneak = Attack MLMer

Early in my network marketing career, I had an issue with rejection due to treatment I experienced during my elementary and middle school years. I was an awkward kid. I had bushy dark eyebrows and huge teeth set in an upper jaw with a tremendous overbite. I also suffered from a fuzzy upper lip, to which I applied Nair one day and chemical-burned the skin below my nose. The next day everyone laughed and asked if it was razor burn. I tried to tell them it was an allergic reaction to mushrooms.

I'm not telling you all this so we can have a pity party with my blast from the past. Believe it or not, those memories actually make me laugh now, and I'm definitely a confident woman who is pleased with how she looks. I used to be embarrassed about how big my teeth were; now my smile is one of my favorite personal features.

We've all grown through a period of time when we were unbearably awkward, and we've all faced our share of rejection as kids. I recently saw a picture of Adam when he was in eighth grade and had a unibrow. Parents must have loving eyes because those puppies, along with all my facial fuzz, should have been plucked! Perhaps this is why as adults we break so easily when we experience rejection in network marketing.

When we get rejected as adults, those same feelings we had when we were being made fun of as kids arise. When our friends laugh at us and tell us to go get real jobs, we're suddenly transported to the front of our eighth-grade math class, feeling like a loser because we've just been picked on by a bunch of mean kids. This is probably why many people find themselves being the "Sneak Attack MLMer" at some point in their career.

So, what are "Sneak Attack MLMers"? They're the people who hide the fact that their company is network marketing. When trying to get people interested, they try to make up another term or talk about it like it's a job. They blanket it with terms fancier than "network marketing," and then people find out it's network marketing after all.

I get it, though. I used to do all those things. I'm going to share with you a time that we were Sneak Attack MLMers. It was early in our career and we had a "not-so-great" idea to post a job opening on Craigslist. That doesn't sound too original right? Maybe so, but here is our angle that made us think we were geniuses at the time. We really wanted to work with people who were bilingual. So the job we posted on Craigslist was asking for a translator. Our master scheme was that the job seekers would need to see our online presentation to really get the "description" of what we were looking for. We figured that we would be able to "hook" them once we got them online. I remember high fiving each other when we thought of the idea. After a whole day of talking to people, we figured out what a waste of time it was. I am sure we looked suspicious to everyone we talked to. We are not proud of that moment, but it was a huge lesson in just being straightforward with your business. They will eventually find out that it is network marketing and if they feel like you were hiding it, they will instantly mistrust you.

Now I don't care what people think, so I just come straight out with it when people ask me what I do. I tell them I'm a network marketing professional. Some people are intrigued and ask questions, while others give me blank stares—and some try to inch away from me like I just passed gas. Their reactions make no difference to me because I now have an unshakable belief in what we do and how much value we bring to the people who are open to receiving it.

Perhaps deep down inside, your scars from past rejection are keeping you from representing network marketing with a badge of honor. Here are some ways to help you through those feelings, as well as some ways to help you represent our profession with boldness and pride in a way that attracts people.

Have skin like a rhinoceros

Learn to become professionally bold. I believe to be successful, you must live your life unoffended and unashamed. Be unashamed of your business, your company, and network marketing. People are attracted to unshakable belief. Be unoffended by people, and extend grace to those who say hurtful things.

If you receive your identity from people, this will be difficult for you. People who draw their identity from the praise of others are the same ones who die from their criticism. Fortune favors the bold! Know who you are and make no apologies for it. Be unashamed to represent your opportunity and extend grace to those who reject your offer (they are not rejecting you personally!).

Remember that it's okay if they don't bite

Let me share a great illustration that has helped us over the years and drives this point home. One of our mentors uses the example of a server offering dessert after a meal. The server visits every table with the famous dessert tray and says, "Hope you saved room for dessert. May I offer you some chunky chocolate cake, cool key lime pie, cheese cake with berries and graham cracker crust, or perhaps the decadent crème brûlée? How about this giant brownie sundae? Looks delicious, doesn't it?"

We've all had the experience where our pant buttons are holding on for dear life and there's absolutely no room for dessert, but everything on that tray looks so good that we can't pass it up. Restaurants know it's a numbers game. Some will order a dessert and some won't, but far more will if they're offered dessert effectively.

The point is, the server's job is to make a compelling offer, and after that it's up to the customer to take action. Could you imagine if you were the server and after you offered the desserts, your guests said, "No way. I hate cake." Would you start crying or quit being a server because it hurt your feelings? Of course not! That would be silly.

Well, the same holds true for this business. Present your offer to as many people as possible, and it too will be a numbers game.[1] Luck does play a small role, but remember that the more you show the plan, the luckier you'll get!

Action Tip: Never end a day with a bad experience. For example, if you're making calls to book appointments, never end the day with that awful feeling you get in your gut when someone rejects your offer. Whenever you have that feeling, push yourself to make another call. Here's why: when you end the day with negative feelings, you'll most likely talk yourself out of making appointments the next day because your body's fight-or-flight mechanism will bring those feelings back. When you end on a good note, you'll be more excited to do the work the next day.

Exercise: Does the fear of rejection overpower you? I have good news and I have bad news. The good news is, you can defeat your fear of rejection; the bad news is, the only way to do it is to get rejected more.

It's never fun to experience rejection, and they say that misery loves company, so get a group of fellow consultants together and have a contest to see who gets to thirty nos the quickest. Do it as a blitz day or over the period of a week, and set an end date so people get moving right away and have a finish line to look forward to. Everyone can chip in for a grand prize to make it fun.

1   McClure, Brian . "Numbers Game, Desserts." Super Saturday. Brian McClure. North Texas Training Center , Irving. 1 June 2011. Lecture

While you're at it, grab a copy of the book *Go For No! Yes is the Destination, No is How You Get There* by Richard Fenton and Andrea Waltz, and get reading.

2

The Secret Agent

The cousin of the "Sneak Attack MLMer" is the "Secret Agent," because both stem from the fear of rejection. Please don't expect me to share yet another embarrassing story of my adolescent rejection. I could share embarrassing anecdotes like the time my mom gave me a perm and turned my hair into a fro, but I think you got the point in the last chapter.

Instead, I'll share a story about a former "Secret Agent." This young woman was new to the big state of Texas, and she felt so far from home and desperately wanted people to like her. She decided to attend a women's conference hosted by an influential church deep in the heart of Texas and had the privilege of getting to know a bright woman while she was there.

During the conference they had many deep conversations and got to know each other well. The young woman shared virtually everything about her life except for her network marketing business. Though she had plenty of opportunities to naturally share about it, she hesitated for fear of what the other woman would think. They exchanged information and kept in touch through social media after the conference.

One day years later, she ran into the woman at a local training center. "I didn't know you were a consultant," the woman said. "I just started this week, and I'm so excited to get my business off the ground." The "Secret Agent" learned a big lesson that day.

As a former "Secret Agent," I had to change my perspective of rejection. What I learned through my years of being in this business, is that rejection is something that I can't take personally. I used to get really upset if someone said no to me, and I know many others also take rejection extremely personally. The fear of rejection is often the one thing that holds people back from having a massive breakthrough in their business.

Here are some guidelines that will help you avoid becoming the "Secret Agent."

Don't take it personally

Through my experiences with rejection, I've learned that the ways individuals react to my offers are based on their past experiences and not my performance (as long as I approach it with the right intentions and with excellence). Recently I called a woman whose business information I had been given. I like to partner with business owners, so I call them to see if they'd be open to having a conversation about a potential partnership.

This woman picked up the phone, and after only seconds of introducing myself, she snapped, "What are you selling? If you're selling something, I'm not interested. I'm sick right now. I'm sick." I politely responded, "I'm sorry to hear you don't feel well and I'm not selling anything, ma'am. I just wanted to... Hello? Hello?" She'd hung up on me.

Remember back in the day when someone would hang up and you could hear the phone slam down onto the receiver? Now you just hear those infamous two beeps. I was rather taken back, because I'd never experienced that type of rudeness, and I found myself so offended that I was huffing and puffing.

Then I started to hear in my spirit that I shouldn't get offended and that I needed to call her back and offer to pray for her. I hesitated to do so but found myself punching her number again.

She picked up the phone, and I said, "Hi, it's Michelle again. I just felt led to call back and see if I can pray for you. I—"

She cut me off with, "No, I'm trying to sleep!" And once again those two beeps sounded in my ear.

I bet you thought she was going to be nice to me after I called back, right? I thought she would have been too. She must've been dealing with something really tough and already wasn't a fan of strangers calling her. The point of the story is, I approached both calls with the right intentions. I truly felt compassion for her.

Honestly, if that had happened to me several years ago, I would have been sobbing in the corner of our home office. However, with more experience I was able to brush it off and continue without a hitch. It's important to detach yourself from the outcome of each interaction.

Jim Rohn says, "You will rarely run into mean people. There are really only ten of them in the world. They just move around a lot."[1] I believe this is true. In my several years of being a network marketing professional, I've rarely run into situations where people are downright mean. In the beginning we experienced it more because we were unknowingly making the mistakes that you're reading about in this book, but once we started to learn from these mistakes and changed our approach, people opened up to us.

This is why we believe in this book! If new people learn to avoid these pitfalls at the start of their career, they'll experience less rejection and more success. Thus, there will be less consultants doing the disappearing act where they're super excited to change their futures and then *boom*, they're never heard from again.

---

1   Jim Rohn. Building Your Network Marketing Business. Video Plus; 1st Edition, 2007. CD.

Understand that sitting on the fence is painful

"Secret Agents" oftentimes are people who don't make a commitment when they partner with a company. They sit on the fence with one leg on the committed side and one leg on the uncommitted side. They usually say they'll try it out, but quit actively building their business after a handful of their friends shoot them down. Then they come back to life when they have an encounter with someone who will be their customer.

We've worked with many "Secret Agents" and fence-sitters, and watching them build their business is like death by paper cuts. It's a slow process for them to quit, and to this day I've never witnessed one of them become successful, because "Secret Agents" aren't willing to do what it takes to have a thriving business.

Don't be open for business only two days a week

If you take your business seriously, it will become a daily part of your life. If you started a clothing store or restaurant but only opened it for a few minutes a week, how successful would you be? I think it would be a simultaneous grand opening and grand closing. "Secret Agents" are not intentional about their business. They only work when it's convenient, and only open up shop when they hear someone mention a need.

Action Tip: Create a daily method of operation for yourself. Have a target number of dials every day. The dials are to make appointments to expose your business. Your DMO can also include how many people on your team you need to reach out to each day and how many pages of a personal development book you should read every day.

Exercise: Track everything you do. Once you create your personal DMO, buy a calendar and write down everything you do every day. For example, if your target dials for the day is ten and you made ten calls, write down 10/10. If you only do eight, then write down 8/10. Tracking your activity will allow you to see holes in your operations.

If you've exposed your business to thirty people or more and no one has become a customer or business partner, you probably need to improve either your follow-up or the validation process. The only way you can improve is to track all your activities. I've done this exercise with many people we mentor, and 95 percent of the time, we find that the lack of results is simply due to lack of action. Numbers don't lie.

3

The Lack Listener

"So, what is the biggest reason you want to join our company?" The man asked me and then glanced at his phone, which sat on the table between us.

As I shared my goals, his eyes glanced around and then brightened. *Did I finally say something interesting?* I wondered. But then he waived his arm, signaling to someone he knew across the restaurant. *I guess not.*

He acted as though everything I said was so uninteresting. "Have you ever done network marketing before?" he asked.

When I started to answer, he cut me off and answered a text. I began again, but before I could finish, he interjected, trying to complete my sentence. *Wow, we have a telepathic on our hands*, I thought. I was getting annoyed simply because I didn't feel like he was listening.

He slipped me an application to get started, and I politely declined. I stood up, threw a glass of ice water in his face, and stormed out of the restaurant. Well, then I snapped back to reality. That part was only a daydream of what I really wanted to do. Nonetheless, he definitely wasn't someone I wanted to work with. Don't be like him.

Here's how you can avoid being the "Lack Listener."

Listen up!

Growing up I was often told, "There's a reason why you have two ears and one mouth." Listening skills are the most important interpersonal skill you can develop. If people don't feel like you listen to them, they won't feel connected to you. With that in mind, if you want people to become your customer or business partner, they need to feel like you're listening; otherwise, they won't feel a personal connection.

Michelle is a terrible multitasker. I know when she's doing something else while we're talking on the phone because I don't feel connected to her since she's really not listening to me. I always think of the scene in *Dumb and Dumber* when Harry and Lloyd are in the bathtub talking about Freida Feltcher. Harry tells Lloyd how Frieda broke up with him by sending him a "John Deere" letter. Lloyd asks him if she gave him any reason for their breakup and he replies, "She gave me a bunch of *lip* for not listening to her or something. I don't know. I wasn't really paying attention." So next time you find yourself not listening, remember this scene or you may get "John Deere" letters from your consultants and prospects.

Making a connection should be important to you

Being able to connect with people is crucial to your success. "Connecting is the ability to identify with people and relate to them in a way that increases your influence with them."[1] There are several facets to making a connection. Of course this includes listening skills, but it also includes being authentic and truly taking an interest in the other person. When you're connecting with people one-on-one, make them feel like they're the only other person in the room. Get rid of distractions, such as your phone.

---

1   John C. Maxwell, *Everyone Communicates, Few Connect: What the Most Effective People Do Differently* (Nashville: Thomas Nelson, 2010), page 3.

Know how to get people to like you

Everyone's favorite subject is him- or herself. If you don't believe us, just scroll through Facebook and look at the flood of selfie pictures. The "selfie revolution" is so rampant that the Selfie Stick was invented. When you take an interest in other people, ask questions and actively listen to their answers. People will instantly like you even though they may know nothing about you.

When you make this kind of connection, you're able to uncover things that are important to people, which you can then use as a way to invite them to take a look at your business. For example, Michelle was talking to a mom at the playground where she takes our daughter. The mom shared with her that she wishes she could find something that will allow her to stay at home with her daughter but still bring in money. That's a perfect opportunity, right? Michelle spent the whole time asking this young mom questions, and through that built trust and discovered a need that she can help her with.

Action Tip: If you tend to get distracted easily, be proactive. For example, if you're meeting someone for a one-on-one over coffee and you love to people watch, position yourself toward to the wall so you won't be tempted to let your attention wander. As well, put your phone on airplane mode, leave it in your car, or turn it off. So many people suffer from what I call "text message anxiety." You're driving in your car or sitting down to a meeting, and your phone vibrates in your pocket. It's so tempting to take a look. Don't do it.

Exercise: The art of connecting with people is a skill that can be developed. Listening skills are a part of the ability to make a true connection with others. Read *Everyone Communicates, Few Connect* by John Maxwell. This is a great book for even seasoned network marketing professionals.

4

The Motor Mouth

Late January. The air was cold and crisp, and the audience teemed with hopeful dreamers as well as first-time guests. A young woman with a bright and bubbly personality had her arm interlocked with the arm of a young man as they approached me. She introduced her rather reluctant guest, and although he managed to say hello, she quickly interrupted and basically began to tell me his life story (seriously, we went way back to his childhood years). I listened and nodded my head, and noticed that he was starting to get a bit uncomfortable—to the point that drops of sweat formed at his hairline.

I tried to interject a few words to put him more at ease, but the young woman began to mix in her life story too. Yes, we were there a *long* time. The young man and I were almost communicating telepathically. I could tell that he wanted out of that conversation; it was like he was blinking *S.O.S.* to me. But did she notice that he was uncomfortable? Did she see how my eyes were starting to glaze over? Not a bit.

Adam always laughs at me because I wear my heart on my sleeve. Whatever I'm thinking always shows up in my facial expressions. So I went into all-out panic mode when this young woman explained how the business works, how the service works, how much it costs, and how we get paid. She talked so fast that all my chances to interrupt were failed attempts. It's probably safe to say that poor young man with the beat-up eardrums did not join that cold January day. I simply couldn't save him from falling victim to yet another "Motor Mouth."

I don't know about you, but sometimes I have a tendency to talk and talk without allowing the awkwardness of silence to creep into a conversation. Perhaps many of you can relate, and that's why the "Motor Mouth" is the most widely made "That Guy" mistake. We need to be mindful that when we speak with someone, we don't talk so much that we miss the entire point of a two-way conversation.

Here are some things to remember the next time you find yourself dominating the conversation with a potential business partner or customer.

Who are you focused on?

When you're talking to people about your business, are you focused on highlighting how great you are or are you focused on their wants and dreams? So many times we think that we need to sell ourselves to gain credibility with potential business partners. Most of the time, they're just trying to figure out if your product, service, or business will solve their problems or bring them what they desire. Focus less on you and the company, and turn your focus to them. If you can uncover their deepest desires and show them how you can help them attain what they want, they will partner with you.

Do you know their wants, dreams and desires?

Listen with your eyes and ears. More than half of human communication is nonverbal. Always watch for clues in people's facial expressions and body language to see if what you're saying is resonating with them. If it's not, ask more questions to uncover what they are passionate about. Even with the most monotone people, expressions and energy change when you talk about their wants and desires.

When in doubt, ask more questions

Don't assume that the topics that are important to you are important to others. I've caught myself constantly talking about the things that I was interested in, not even thinking that others may not deem them equally important. Give people the answers they're interested in, and if you don't know those answers, then ask more questions.

Use the tools, don't be the tool

Allow your company tools, such as videos, to do the explaining for you. Many people need visuals to effectively internalize what you are saying. When you attempt to explain how everything works, you're giving them only enough information to make an uneducated decision. A key phrase that you can use is, "It's 99 percent visual. If I try to explain it, it'll take twice as long and I'll just confuse you."

Be the messenger, not the message

The most important reason to use the company tools is to ensure duplication. This point is especially important for those I like to call the "Uber Successful." I've had the opportunity to work with a lot of high-caliber individuals—from doctors, to lawyers, to people who have hugely successful brick-and-mortar businesses.

The most common pitfall I've seen when coaching the "Uber Successful" is that they want to reinvent the wheel and make it much more complicated than it should be. Every time this happens, they stifle their team's ability to grow rapidly, because what they do is difficult for the average person to duplicate. Darren Hardy said it best in his audiobook *Making the Shift: Your First 7 Days*: "If your mouth is moving, you better be pointing to a tool."[1]

---

1   Darren Hardy, *Making the Shift: Your First 7 Days* MP3.

Even if you're a smooth talker and great presenter, if your business is personality driven and not systems driven, you won't create duplication. Early on in our business, when we would sit down with potential business partners, we would show them the entire company PowerPoint. We got really good at it and began closing more and more consultants. Then our team started asking us to go to appointments with them and do the presentation. We found that the only time new consultants were joining our team was when we were doing the presentation!

Now we show the company video every time, and we teach our team to do the same. We knew we hit duplication when we went on vacation off-grid and then returned to find that several new consultants had joined our team.

Always remember: It doesn't matter what works; it only matters what duplicates.[2]

Don't let it slip

While we are on the topic of conversation, I must add the importance of cleaning up your speech. I've been a part of some meetings where, although we were in a professional setting, people were dropping "F-bombs" galore.

In network marketing, your fellow teammates and company mates become your best friends and sometimes even closer than family. Since we get that comfortable, some people let their language become a little loose. Within the context of personal branding, the way you speak, including the words you choose, paints a picture of who you are. Leaders who use inappropriate language are perceived as less credible, even among their peers. As well, it's a good idea to clean up your speech anyway so you don't offend anyone, whether in the business or personal realm.

---

2   Eric Worre, *Go Pro – 7 Steps to Becoming a Network Marketing Professional* (Network Marketing Pro, Inc., 2013), page 69.

Know when to stop talking and go in for the kill

I've seen many people get talked out of joining an opportunity because the "Motor Mouth" habit takes over. So often a prospect reviews a presentation and is ready to get started, but the "Motor Mouth" thinks he or she needs to give out every fact, detail, and pie chart about their company! A few minutes later, the prospect decides that it sounds too complicated and says no to the opportunity. I myself have had times where I talked people right out of joining. I constantly have to remind myself that "the less you say, the more you make."

Action Tip: If you have the tendency to talk over people (yes, yes, we know it's because you're excited, but stop it!), mute your phone when it isn't your time to talk. This will keep you from interrupting the prospect. You will then need to manually unmute your phone, which will give you an extra second to think twice about your response.

I like to use a headset and hold my phone while talking; that way I have access to the mute button. This protects my prospects from background noises such as my hungry cats or crying toddler, as well as shields them from me talking too much.

Exercise: Ask a trusted leader's opinion and have them rate your listening skills. Find a leader who will tell you the truth, not just what you want to hear. Just be sure you're prepared to take the constructive criticism and use it to improve. If you know that any feedback outside of someone telling you, "You're amazing" will crush you, then personal development needs to become your new best friend.

5

The Social Media Spammer

I was probably one of the last people on earth to open a Facebook account. I think Adam's grandmother even had one before I did. I didn't have MySpace when that was popular either, so I was definitely behind on social media. I finally opened my Facebook account about a year after we started our -business, and at the time, I thought it was the greatest tool to get people to join our team! Little did I know that I looked like a tool instead, because I was using social media to promote my business completely wrong.

Join my team! Get paid while you sleep! I can save you money, and we can make money with the greatest opportunity of all time! Private message me for details! This was what I would often blast out onto everyone's news feed several times a day. I would keep checking back to see if I had any activity on my posts. Any likes? No. Any comments? Nope. Hmmm, no one private-messaged me. I'll check back in ten minutes; maybe everyone is busy at work and not looking at Facebook (which we both know is a lie—everyone is looking at their Facebook feed, even the ones sitting on the toilet).

If I was completely honest with myself, people didn't like, comment, or message me because they were getting annoyed with my spamming and selling tactics. My Facebook wall was a stream of self-centered "me, me, me, this is what I want" posts that didn't add value to those following me. Instead, I had become "That Guy" on social media and had several people un-follow and un-friend me. How do I know? Well, one day, I looked up someone who I was friends with, but we were no longer friends.

Lucky for you, you can learn from my mistakes. Here are some tips on how to use social media properly so you don't get the un-friend, un-follow, or block button clicked on your page.

Include a variety of posts

Limit your posts about your business to one or two a day. Share about different fun events that you're attending with your company. Upload pictures with people on your team and different leaders. Make sure you include posts on what you're doing and enjoying outside your business life, because the people who care about you care about all of that too.

When you used to watch TV (notice the past tense—you're in business now, you don't have time to watch TV), did you pay close attention to the commercials or did you tune out? You most likely tuned out, unless it was a Carl's Jr. commercial. People don't want to be pitched and sold your products, especially when they're trying to relax.

A large portion of my friends on Facebook are in network marketing, and I noticed that my feed was becoming a long line of sales pitches with a few lifestyle posts in between. When people pitch on social media, it looks like a bunch of commercials, which will make your contacts skim past your posts and tune you out.

When I see commercial-type posts on social media, my imaginary alarm bells go off, waving big red flags to warn me "That Guy" is spamming my news feed again. If you're going to post about your business, make sure the majority of your posts showcase lifestyle. When you add pictures that depict a lifestyle of fun events and gatherings, people will become curious about what you do. We've had many people contact us to find out about our business just because of our lifestyle updates, pictures, positive posts, and quotes. People love to associate themselves with people who know where they're going.

Keep it G rated

If you use social media as a tool for your business, avoid posting content that is negative, sexual, or morally questionable (for example, party/drunk pictures). You're an extension of your company. In fact, even if you're not with a particular company, you're representing the brand of the most important company, which is You, Incorporated.

How do you want people to see you? What you write in your posts, what kind of pictures you upload, and even the articles and content you share is a reflection of you. All of this will affect your credibility and may determine if people will partner with you or not. Instead, post motivating quotes and articles or industry-specific content that provides value. Just remember that social media can be very powerful if you use it correctly. It can also work against you if you don't. Always ask yourself, "How can I add value to the people following me today?"

Use social media to be social

Social media is also a great tool to reconnect with people you've lost touch with. Be sure to take some time to rebuild those relationships, especially if you had a close friendship in the past. Many people are trained to dump all their contacts in the funnel by directly pitching all of them as soon as possible. While some of that advice may be good, it's important to use your instincts and make the decision to build rapport or reconnect with certain people.

It all boils down to the classic Golden Rule. If your childhood best friend found you on Facebook and immediately started to pitch you his or her business, how would that make you feel? So take time and enjoy rebuilding the relationship. Don't go straight for the pitch. That will seem too "salesy" and insincere for making the connection.

Make it personal

Don't use Facebook invites for home meetings/parties. Make it personal with a phone call. I have missed many Facebook events that I didn't even know I was invited to. Others I didn't respond to because I believed if it was important enough, the host would have contacted me personally.

Let's face it, we make time for the things that are important to us (keyword "us"). People are very guarded with their time because they have so many choices of where to invest themselves. I laugh when I think about this, because I picture people scrolling through their messages, telling their friends they're busy, when meanwhile they're slumped on the couch, reaching their hand into a big bag of Flamin' Hot Cheetos while watching another rerun of Maury Povitch.

Here's an example. Friends invite you to their home for a grand opening of their new business. You know you should attend out of respect for them, but it's not the same feeling you would get if you were invited to box seats at the Super Bowl. You're not that excited to go. Is it easier to not respond to an e-mail or Facebook message, or is it easier to say no to them while you're on the phone with them? If you use e-mail, a private message, an Evite, or a Facebook event invitation, people will pretend they didn't see it or will look for any excuse not to attend.

I would compare this example to moving. You find out who your friends are when it comes time to move. Just like you find out who your friends are when it comes time to support and hear about your business. If you send them a message through social media, it's easier for them to escape with any excuse not to help you move. However, if you call them and tell them they could be your hero and you would love them forever, that will increase their chances of saying yes because it's more difficult to say no when they're having a live conversation with you.

Action Tip: Make your posts more interactive by asking for suggestions. For example, if you're traveling to an event you can post *I'm traveling to*

Chicago next month for business. What are some great restaurants and/or must-visit sites? These types of posts will generate the curiosity that will cause people to ask what you do.

Exercise: Don't make your pitch or invitation through a private message. Always use technology as a means to make an appointment and then make your invitation over the phone. Here's the type of message you can send if your initial contact will be through social media or text: *Hey Susan, I want to touch base about something I'm working on and want to run it by you to see if you can connect me with the right people. When do you have five minutes in the next few days for a quick call?*

Also, when I'm coaching people who are new to network marketing, I find they always have many people on social media whom they don't have phone numbers for. This is a great script to use to get their phone numbers. People like being connectors, and most people are willing to help you and will give you their phone number and time.

6

The "Oh, by the Way" Phone Caller

I felt my phone vibrating in my pocket. It had been a tough couple of days, plus the night before I'd had a dream that Adam was flirting with Jamie Lee Curtis. Then I woke up late for an important phone appointment, only to step in my cat's hairball-beef-and-gravy stomach concoction as I stumbled out of bed to pull out my phone. I definitely didn't feel like having a business call, but when I looked at my caller ID, I breathed a sigh of relief. On it was the name of a dear friend who I had not spoken to in quite some time.

Maybe a conversation with her will cheer me up a bit, I thought to myself. *Let's see what she's been up to.* I answered, and my day brightened as we chatted and caught up. Then about fifteen minutes into the phone call, she inserted the phrase, "Oh, by the way…" and started down a long path of explaining her new business and how the products were amazing and how I needed to join her because they were going to make a lot of money. An icky feeling arose in my gut, and my happiness suddenly disappeared as I wondered if that was the *only* reason she gave me a call.

It may seem like common sense to call a friend and catch up before you spring the invitation to look at your business, especially if this is a friend you haven't talked to in a while. It may seem insincere to just call them and get to the point of your call right away. However, this is a situation where common sense actually creates an opposite effect. If you call a friend, spend time catching up, and then say, "Oh, by the way" and transition into your spiel, your friend is going to think the first part of the conversation was insincere.

Here are some ways to call a friend who you would like to invite to take a look at your business, without the risk of looking like the "'Oh, by the Way' Phone Caller."

It's been a while since we've talked

If your friend is one you haven't talked to in a while, call and apologize for not being able to keep in touch. Mention that you want to run something by him or her because it's important to you and then get right to the point. We're all super busy. Apologizing for not keeping in touch and then getting straight to the point is more appreciated than the "oh, by the way" approach.

Take the time to rebuild rapport

Simply call with the intention to just catch up. If the friend asks what you've been up to, mention your business but say that you can talk about it another time. Then get back to asking questions about him or her. You can always circle back later and invite him or her to have coffee to talk more about your exciting new venture.

It's important to use your judgment for each contact. Friends who were really close in the past may need some time to just catch up and rebuild the connection before talking with you about your business. Acquaintances are easier to get straight to the point with.

You popped into my mind

Say, "I've just started a new business and it made me think of you." You can also say that you remember him or her being super motivated and that this opportunity may be of interest. Just be mindful that when you use the "Direct Approach,"[1] you may run into people who will tell you they're too busy to add anything more to their plate or that they're not open to an opportunity.

Action Tip: Set up a time restraint to avoid the risk of catching up if you want to go straight for the invitation. You can mention that you only have a minute but wanted to call and get feedback on something that's important to you. This will help you avoid the small talk that could potentially become a catching-up session.

Exercise: Inviting people to take a look at your business so they can confidently refer the right person creates a win–win situation. Since more people will look at your business, you'll naturally gain more business partners. If friends are interested, they'll say so; if they're not, they can still connect you with the right people.

Instead of directly asking your contacts if they're open to making money or if they want to try your weight loss product or vitamins, tweak it by saying, "I'm not sure if what I'm doing would be of interest to you (or I'm not sure if my products would be something you'd be interested in). Can you do me a favor and take a look at it so you can feel confident in referring me to someone you know who may be the right fit?" Just remember that your main focus is to get them to take a look, not to get them to join. This "Indirect Approach" will ensure that their walls don't go up.[2]

---

1   Eric Worre, *Go Pro – 7 Steps to Becoming a Network Marketing Professional* (Network Marketing Pro, Inc., 2013), page 51.

2   Eric Worre, *Go Pro – 7 Steps to Becoming a Network Marketing Professional* (Network Marketing Pro, Inc., 2013), page 53.

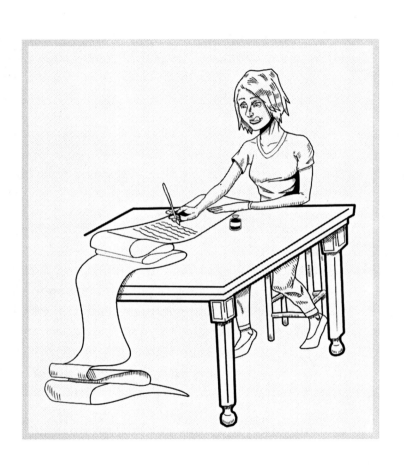

7

The Long-Winded Writer

We arrived home from our first company convention, and I was so excited by the whole experience (if you've ever attended a national convention, you know what I mean). We were given "homework" to sit down and make calls immediately after the convention, so I got my list of contacts, dug my phone out of my purse, and sat down at our pub table.

Suddenly, I slipped the phone back into my purse pocket as I completely chickened out. *Aha! I know. I'll e-mail everyone instead*, I thought. *There's no way I can call all these people on a Sunday, so I'll go ahead and write them a nice e-mail.* Well, that nice e-mail turned into a nice, *long* e-mail. My little fingers just kept tapping away at my keyboard. Before long I had a dissertation on my hands. I took my mouse, pointed the arrow on the Send button, and off it went.

I believe people who fear the phone, like I did, resort to sending e-mails because the rejection is not as direct. It's not as hard to swallow if people don't answer our e-mails or if they reply no. It's a bit harder to take when people tell us no in person or over the phone. So to avoid it, people send their entire spiel in an e-mail.

Here are some things to remember so you don't become the "Long-Winded Writer."

Keep in mind that less is more!

If an e-mail or a text's content doesn't grab a person's attention in the first few seconds, it might as well say "yadda, yadda, yadda," because that's what your prospect is seeing or (most likely) not even reading. Michelle won't even read e-mails from me if they're more than a few lines. After the first couple of lines, she's already moved on to the next e-mail. She says if the subject is important enough, I'll tell her via a phone call or in person, which also holds true for your prospects. If something is important enough, be sure to tell them personally.

If you have an analytical mind or green personality (if you're familiar with the color personalities), you most likely struggle in this area. You thrive on lots of information, but please, for the love of everyone's overwhelmed inbox, remember that not all of us love lots of information. Some of us want to cut right to the chase. The people who want more information will let you know.

Face your fear of the phone

If you feel the need to only send e-mails, that might indicate that you have a fear of the phone. The only way I know to overcome this particular fear is to simply face it head on. No matter how great the fear may be, make the phone call anyway. The more phone calls you make, the less fearful you'll be.

Michelle used to really fear the phone. She would lock herself in the closet and make her calls because she didn't want me or anyone else to hear her mess up. Now she doesn't even think twice about making a phone call. The only fear I need to help her with now is her fear of birds. Perhaps I'll just happen to let a wild turkey into our house one morning since she needs to face it head on.

Action Tip: When I get nervous, I forget what I'm supposed to say. Before I know it, I'm blabbing down other rabbit trails. It may sound silly, but writing out scripts and strictly adhering to the script will dramatically help until your invitation is cemented in your mind. Make sure to add in "ahs" and "ums" so it doesn't sound like you're reading it off a paper. Refer to the "Oh, by the Way Phone Caller" for the script that we use.

Exercise: If you need help increasing your confidence in making phone calls, write out a simple script and practice it with your upline or a business partner. Once you feel more assured, make your first call. This will help ensure that you don't go into your first few calls "cold."

8

The Bait and Slammer

The boxing match between Manny Pacquio and Antonio Margarito was an expensive and highly coveted fight on Pay-Per-View. As they got ready to duke it out for the WBC Super Welter Weight Championship, people were filling up the house. Doorbell ring after doorbell ring, both living rooms were packed with people. The smell of pepperoni pizza filled the house, and everyone salivated at getting their hands on a couple of slices.

We called everyone into one room. It was almost like herding cattle. "Okay, everyone, thank you so much for coming," I said. "Before we all grab a plate and watch the fight, I wanna share with you a great business opportunity that I found." Suddenly, everyone's arms folded and their excited expressions hardened.

That was not one of our shining moments. We did the presentation—and super-fast, might I add, so we didn't get murdered. The good news was, a couple people actually joined. The bad news was, we lost an opportunity with the rest of the bunch by giving a bad first impression. They probably thought, *If I have to bait and slam my friends to do this business, I'm out!* That was one of our greatest rookie mistakes.

Here's how to set up a home presentation or meeting properly, so you don't end up looking like the "Bait and Slammer."

Know that home presentations are a homerun

Some people don't like home presentations. I think they're effective because they're super personal. Most people will show up to a home before they'll show up to a hotel; therefore, your exposure rate is higher. If you're implementing home presentations or plan to, be sure that you're upfront with your purpose of getting together. Otherwise, you'll be tagged as the "Bait and Slammer."

Let the main thing be the main thing

Always be upfront with your guests and explain the main reason for your meeting. Let them know that the purpose of getting together is for you to share your business with them so they'll know how they can support you in your journey.

We always train our team to invite their friends and family with the intention that they're simply coming to learn how they can be supportive in the business. We don't pressure anyone to purchase anything or join, saying, "In fact, you can leave your wallet at home." With this laid-back posture, more people attend because the pressure is taken off. The more people who attend, the greater the probability of gaining customers, business partners, or both.

People are jaded by the high-pressure approach. Taking the pressure off will ensure that you'll have lasting customers and the right business partners, because you're allowing them to make the decision out of pure desire and not a guilt-trip.

Don't provide an elaborate meal

You can have refreshments, but don't let the food be the center of your presentation. I've been to presentations where the meal was the center and it took forever to get people to pay attention to the presentation. I think some people came simply to have a nice meal and then left when the presentation started. Others left because the presentation started too late. Another reason to stay away from a big spread is it's not easy to duplicate. Some of your guests will instantly decline your opportunity because of the time and money they assume needs to be invested. If people don't think they can do what you do, they won't even try. That's also a great reason not to present the material yourself without using company tools such as DVDs and online videos to present your opportunity. You might be a polished presenter with a high batting average but again if people don't think they can do what you do, they won't.

Be honest about coffee and one-on-one meetings

The same rules apply when you're setting up a coffee or one-on-one meeting. Make sure that if you're asking people to meet you, they know the purpose of the meeting. They don't need to know all the information beforehand, just that you'll be sharing your business. Also, if your upline or a fellow leader will be joining you, make sure your prospect knows that as well. Nothing makes someone put up a wall faster than the "closer" unexpectedly showing up.

Action Tip: If you or someone on your team is close to a promotion, have a "home presentation blitz," where you have several home presentations scheduled in a row and invite more people than you normally would in your regular daily method of operation. You can get people emotionally enrolled in helping with the promotion by creating a buzz around the purpose of the events. Having a prize for the "one-hundredth customer" and a celebration when the promotion happens will make it fun and engaging for everyone who participates.

Exercise: Many people shy away from exposing their "hot market" to their network marketing business. The "hot market," which is family members and closest friends, can also be the hardest critics we will face, and a grand opening done right can increase success.

If you haven't had a grand opening for your network marketing business yet, now is the time to do it. It's the perfect low-pressure (or even no-pressure) way to expose even your toughest critics. Have them come and look for you, and tell them to leave their wallets at home. So many people feel the pressure to buy when their loved ones start a network marketing business. When people feel pressured, they go into hiding. The point of you sharing your business is to get supporters and advocates. The more people who are out there referring you, the better your business will do in the long run.

9

Negative Nancy and Poor-Me Paul

I arrived at our local presentation with my hands full of sign-in sheets and name tags. It was raining, and as we set up the table, thunder rolled outside. An older woman walked up and greeted us. With a stern look on her face, she started to complain about the weather. I tried not to allow her negativity get to me, especially since I've always liked big storms, and didn't want to let her be a kill-joy.

I continued to set up the projector and screen as I listened to her. She followed me around and complained about how she wasn't getting any help. "We just had a training last week. Were you there?" I asked. She replied, "No, I couldn't find a ride." Instantly, I knew where this conversation was going.

"What about public transportation? The bus stop is right at the corner of the parking lot," I continued. She answered, "Well, my sponsor isn't helping me and that's why I didn't have any money for the bus and couldn't buy a training ticket." Again, she dodged responsibility. As minutes of my life were being sucked away, more people filed into the room.

I pulled her aside and let her know it wasn't a good time to talk about her struggles since guests were in the room, and then advised her to wait until after the presentation. "Fine," she huffed, rolling her eyes, and then plopped herself down in the front row. I could've sworn that I saw a plume of dust fly into the air, but that could have just been her dirty attitude.

Getting stuck talking to a "Negative Nancy" or a "Poor-Me Paul" is like being vacuumed into an energy-sucking vortex that spins you around, makes you nauseated, and spits you out on the floor curled up in the fetal position. Maybe that's a little dramatic (and sorry if your name is Nancy or Paul), but it is draining to talk to someone who always sees the glass as half empty or thinks the sky is falling.

It's important to make sure that you're not "Negative Nancy" or "Poor-Me Paul," because no one will enjoy working with you or want to join your team. The "Negative Nancys" and "Poor-Me Pauls" have one thing in common: they like to evade responsibility. They believe everything happens to them, instead of realizing that their situations are a result of the choices they make—just like the woman who believed her lack of success was her sponsor's fault. We could have titled this chapter "The Blamer" or "The Complainer". The fact is that a negative attitude is the underlying issue of people who blame others for their lack of success or complain about their circumstances.

People Need to Willingly Follow

Oftentimes I get into coaching sessions with people, and they wonder why they're not successful in building a team and why they struggle in getting help from other leaders. Let's address the first problem, which is getting people to willingly follow you.

Leadership is critical in network marketing, because it takes true leadership and not positional leadership. John Maxwell talks about this in his book *The 5 Levels of Leadership: Proven Steps to Maximize Your Potential.* The first level is positional leadership. At this level, you don't need leadership skills; people have to follow you because you have a leadership position. An example of this would be a horrible manager who you have to follow because not doing so could cost you your job. You're not inspired to follow them; you do it out of obligation.

Network marketing takes leadership skills, because people need to willingly follow you. For them to stick around, you need to be able to cast vision and empower them to develop the skills. First, you attract people with your positive, encouraging attitude and then you solidify the relationship by having a strong foundation of leadership.

Second, no one wants to work with people who always act like the sky is falling. We do feel like we have an obligation to help everyone who joins our team, but the "Poor-Me Pauls" get their phone calls returned after those who don't have a perpetually negative attitude.

It may sound harsh, but here's my reasoning: "Poor-Me Pauls" are rarely coachable. They want to complain just to hear their own whiny voices in hopes that someone will pat their back and lick their wounds. I do that enough with my cat; I don't need to spend time doing that with an uncoachable business partner, and you shouldn't either. Have sympathy for those who are struggling (this business isn't always easy), but make sure they're open to your coaching and actually take strides to improve before you continue to invest your time in them.

Here's how to ensure you never get tagged as a "Negative Nancy" or a "Poor-Me Paul."

Smile while you talk

No matter what country you're in, a smile has a universal meaning. When you smile at people, it gives them an opportunity to open up to you. If you're not used to smiling, practice until it comes naturally. The last thing you want is to creep people out with a fake smile.

Change your words

Instead of saying "I have to," say, "I get to." It will change your attitude toward any task.

- "I get to make calls today."
- "I get to follow up with prospects today."
- "I get to go to a meeting."
- "I get to speak on a conference call."
- "I get to…" (You get the idea.)

Watch what you ingest

I'm not talking about what you eat. I'm talking about what you feed your mind. If you're constantly watching reality shows that showcase scandalous interactions between people or watching talk shows that have guests in the perceptual state of negativity, you'll start to develop a negative state of mind. Whatever you feed your mind is what will naturally come out when you talk with other people.

We never watch the news on purpose. Have you noticed that when you watch the news, all you can think or talk about are the negative things you see? I can tell when people are news watchers because they like to talk about the bad events happening in our world. While we shouldn't be completely ignorant about current events, be purposeful in guarding your mind. For every bad event happening in the world, there are positive ones that go unnoticed every day. Which events are you focused on?

Fight against the zombie apocalypse

"Some people are dead already. They just haven't made it official yet."[1] I always giggle when I hear John Maxwell say this. There's so much truth to it. Michelle has a recurring dream that she's fighting zombies. One time she told me that the weapon in her dream was a water gun. We

---

[1]   Maxwell, John . "Ambition." Ambit Energy Conference, American Airlines Center, Dallas. 1 Sept. 2012. Lecture.

tried to figure out why she kept having these dreams and came to the conclusion that the zombies symbolize her daily interactions with people who live life without passion.

So many people work a job or even own a small business and have no passion or purpose for it; they do it for a paycheck. We've found that, as human beings, the longer that people live outside of feeling purposeful, the more cynical they become. It's so important that we figure out where our strength zone and passion cross. If you can find a way to incorporate it into your daily life, you're not in danger of being infected by the zombie virus.

Cultivate an attitude of gratitude

When you cultivate an attitude of constant thankfulness, it's impossible to become a "Negative Nancy" or "Poor-Me Paul." Our friend and business partner suffered a brain injury several years ago, and despite the challenges she faces on a daily basis, she's always upbeat and thankful. "Pity parties are no fun because you are often alone and there are no refreshments."[2] Whenever we find ourselves having a pity party, we stop and list all the things we're thankful for. The result is that we no longer have a bad attitude.

Know that your attitude and your success go hand in hand

I recently read an article in *SUCCESS* magazine that stated the biggest factor in determining one's success is a positive attitude. Success takes perseverance. People don't simply arrive at the doorstep of success. They have to work at it through the peaks and valleys of the journey.

Perseverance and a bad attitude are like oil and vinegar. They don't go together. A negative attitude is always a precursor to quitting. When people we work with succumb to a bad attitude, it's only a matter of

---

2   Carter, Joey. "Wisdom of Mary Crowley." Super Saturday. Brian McClure. North Texas Training Center, Irving . 1 June 2011. Lecture.

time before they close the door on their dreams. On the other hand, a positive attitude is that inner voice that keeps cheering you on. It tells you to keep pushing forward and that success will happen in due time.

I love biographies about individuals who have beaten insurmountable odds. I notice that they all have one thing in common, and that's the ability to have a positive outlook even in the darkest of times.

Action Tip: Do you have "Negative Nancys" or "Poor-Me Pauls" on your team? Give them an assignment that will improve their results and have them get back to you when it's complete. You can even set a deadline. Some will take your coaching and others will not, and that's how you determine who gets your precious time.

Exercise: How do you determine if you're a "Negative Nancy" or "Poor-Me Paul?" Take a week and really listen to how you speak. A mentor of ours had us go through an eye-opening exercise where we stuck a handful of pennies in one pocket and every time we thought or said something negative, we had to transfer a penny to the other pocket. I was surprised by how many negative thoughts took hold in my mind and how much I complained.

The Bible says, "Life and death are in the power of the tongue" (Proverbs 18:21) and it also describes the tongue as a small rudder that can steer a huge ship.[3] The words you speak greatly affect the direction of your life, in part because those words can attract or repel the people around you. Your success in network marketing is all about people.

---

3   *Proverbs. The Maxwell Leadership Bible.* 2nd Vers. Vol. 1. Nashville: Thomas Nelson, 1982. Print.

10

The Nose Deaf and Disheveled

Adjusting to life with our newborn daughter left us in love but extremely sleep deprived. She was our first baby, and one morning I was running on maybe three hours of sleep since she was feeding every two hours on the dot and neither Adam nor I could get the swaddling thing down. I woke up and stumbled into the kitchen, then handed off our precious little screamer to my mom, who had been helping us adjust to our new season of life.

"I'm out of Hazelnut Coffee-Mate! I cannot function without coffee, and I cannot drink my coffee without my Hazelnut Coffee-Mate!" I was on the verge of losing it. Though I was tired and definitely didn't care what I looked like, I got my shoes and rallied Adam to drive me to the store. Notice that I just put on my shoes and left—wearing baggy sweats and a tee shirt that had spit-up stains adorning my front and shoulders. My hair was still in a bun.

Fast-forward to the store, where I was having a conversation with a sharply put together woman while in line. As we wrapped up a short rapport-building session, I offered my card. Her eyes moved over me from head to toe as if she was secretly sizing me up, then she took the card and I never heard from her again. I had "first-impression failure."

First impressions are extremely important. If you're reading this, I'm assuming you have a network marketing business, which is basically a business of attraction. The people who have mastered creating their own personal brand do the best in network marketing because they have a way of attracting people to them. People don't buy into your company statistics or track record; instead, they buy into you.

At times, I've been at company events or local presentations where I saw consultants who looked like they just rolled out of bed, painted their house, and decided to come to a meeting. I actually have compassion for them because they are typically the ones who struggle in network marketing even though they try the hardest.

One time I was talking to an unkempt woman who tried very hard to succeed in her business, and she told me that whenever she gave out her flyer (which is not what we train people to do, by the way), people just handed it right back to her. She was experiencing a lot of rejection, and I felt deep compassion for her.

However, if someone is going to talk to people about making money or creating their dream life, they must have a polished look. I don't mean wearing a custom-tailored designer suit or holding a Fendi purse. What I mean by polished is hair brushed, teeth brushed, and nice makeup for the women and neatly trimmed facial hair for the men.

When I first started out in network marketing, I didn't know about the power of personal branding or that I should treat my network marketing business like it was a real business. Instead of dressing for success, I would show up to presentations and events wearing torn jeans and a hat. Luckily, one of my mentors pulled me aside and talked to me about it. When I cleaned up my look, I began to perform differently in my business. I saw myself as a professional, and when I started to see myself differently, I started to perform better and have better results.

It may seem basic, but just remember that deodorant, neat and clean clothes, and a pack of breath strips in your pocket go a long way. I'll list some tips geared toward the women, then Adam will provide some tips for the men, and then we'll give some tips that apply to both genders.

Have a polished look that makes a statement (without a credit card statement)

If you want to step it up a notch, business casual or even a nicely put together but laid-back look will send the message that you're professional. In the beginning, we didn't have disposable income to go out and buy new wardrobes. We focused on reinvesting our profits back into our business and into personal development, so I went to resale stores. I still love them because you can find a lot of unique pieces to mix into your wardrobe.

Beautiful hair doesn't have to get you into debt

Are you in need of a hairstyle but don't have a lot of money to spend? Book an appointment at a beauty school and allow a student to cut or color your hair. Students are under the supervision of their teachers, so they do a great job. A simple cut usually ranges from twelve to fifteen dollars. If funds are tight, go for a hairstyle that doesn't require a lot of maintenance like highlights or fresh layers every couple of weeks. Just make sure your style is clean and professional.

Makeup is easier than you think

Use YouTube to learn how to put on makeup, and Ulta has a great selection of inexpensive makeup brands. You may be thinking that this section seems a little shallow, but if we're honest, by human nature we're all a little bit shallow. People use first impressions to make snap decisions about you and your business. If they don't see you as professionally put together, you may risk losing a chance to get them interested in your business.

Those were tips for the women, so I'm going to step aside and let Adam speak to the men.

Look the part

When Michelle and I started our business we were twenty-three and twenty-five years old. Most days you would find me in shorts, flip flops, a tee shirt, and a hat (and I still dress like that around the house). When I was out and about, people were constantly asking me where I went to school. "I don't go to school," I would tell them in a rather defensive manner. "I have a business!" It annoyed me until I looked in the mirror one day and decided that, if I were them, I wouldn't take me seriously either. It was time to suit up and show up.

Leaders are always dressed above average because they are *never* average. Learn to observe. If you go to your company's national convention or regional trainings, look at your top leaders. What are they wearing? How do they carry themselves? If you're attending in a tee shirt because you think, *Hey, I'm not speaking. If I was, I would have dressed up*, then you're not treating your business seriously. One of my mentors, Joey Carter, once shared "You have to see it before you see it or you will never see it."[1] I promise that if you take yourself seriously, others will too.

Suit up and shine your shoes

Buy at least one inexpensive suit (look for sales—you don't have to break the bank). If you can only afford one, blue or black works great because you can buy different slacks and shirts to mix it up and create different looks. Sharp professional men will take notice of shirts, watches, and shoes. Again, these don't have to be super expensive or name brand. Also, make sure you shine your dress shoes. Polished shoes are another thing that successful men look at when they're "sizing up" other men. Polished shoes are like a coat of honor; if a man has polished shoes, he is someone to do business with.

And here are some final tips for both genders.

---

1   Carter, Joey. "Wisdom of Mary Crowley." Super Saturday. Brian McClure. North Texas Training Center, Irving . 1 June 2011. Lecture.

Combine humbleness and class

Many people think network marketing produces only hobby money. I always knew there was huge money in network marketing, and my eyes were opened even more after I attended my first Go Pro network marketing event. I met people making ridiculous amounts of money, and they all had these two traits in common: they were humble and professionally put together.

Raise your leadership lid

One of the biggest eye-openers for me on this topic happened during a Saturday training hosted by our #1 income earner. He asked the audience, "Who here wished they had recruited me?" Of course, everyone's hands shot up (I think I raised both hands and one leg to make sure I got noticed). He then said, "Okay, do you want to know the secret?" Everyone sat up straight and leaned forward waiting for the silver bullet. He said, "If you want to recruit me, you have to become me."

Now that's a pretty bold statement to make, and some may think it's pretty cocky too. The reality he was trying to get across was not to sound cocky but rather to be confident in his leadership. You tend to attract people who match your level of leadership and below. This leader was referring to what John Maxwell calls the "Law of the Lid," from his best-selling book *The 21 Irrefutable Laws of Leadership*.

The Law of the Lid states that "leadership ability determines a person's level of effectiveness."[2] The lower an individual's ability to lead, the lower the lid on his or her potential; the higher the individual's ability to lead, the higher the lid on his or her potential. To give you an example, if your leadership rates an 8, then you will never attract someone that rates greater than a 7. If your leadership level is a 4, you will not attract someone higher than a 3. "Your leadership ability, for better or for worse,

---

2   John C. Maxwell, *The 21 Irrefutable Laws of Leadership* (Nashville: Thomas Nelson, 2007), page 1.

always determines your effectiveness and the potential impact of your organization."[3]

So in order for you to recruit someone like our #1 income earner who has been in the trenches for decades—learning, growing, and leading—you need to raise your leadership lid dramatically in order to attract someone of that caliber into your business.

Realize that we all make snap judgments, whether we like it or not

Do you like to people watch? If you do, you probably ask yourself questions like, "What does he do for a living?" and "What's her story?" We all size each other up in a matter of seconds. My favorite place to people watch is the airport. There's always a wide assortment of people, and we've all seen those who have caught our curiosity because of the way they dressed or carried themselves.

People are watching you too. How do you carry yourself? Are you confident? Do you walk around with your head down? Do you smile easily and make eye contact with people? These are a few questions to ask yourself, because the way you carry yourself makes an impact on whether or not you're able to attract the right people.

Don't let your breath smell like garlic and cumin

Invest in an extra toothbrush! I always carry a toothbrush and toothpaste in my computer bag so when I'm out and about, I can always freshen up, especially before meetings. By far the best way to turn off prospects is to saturate them with a horrific combination of coffee, onions, and garlic on your breath. Trust me, it doesn't matter how smooth you are; if your breath causes eyes to water, it's game over! Don't be "That Guy"!

---

3   John C. Maxwell, *The 21 Irrefutable Laws of Leadership* (Nashville: Thomas Nelson, 2007), page 1.

Action Tip: If nothing else, take a shower and brush your teeth!

Exercise: List five characteristics of your ideal business partner.[4] Ours are *integrity, hard-working, positive, a team player,* and *coachable.* Now evaluate yourself and determine if you embody the characteristics you just listed. Once you embody those characteristics, you'll attract the right people to join your team.

4   Ray Montie, "Finding Pearls," Powertrip Conference, 2014.

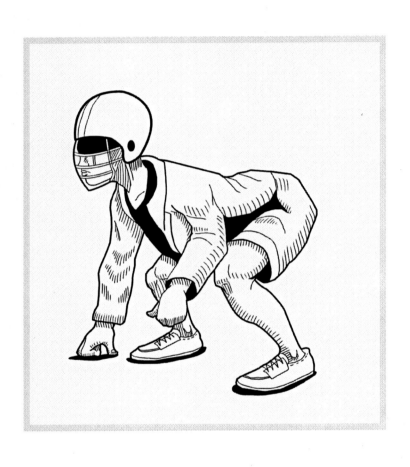

11

The Defensive Tackler

The presentation I was attending with a guest ended, and I turned to him and asked, "So what do you think?" (By the way, it's a rookie mistake to phrase a follow-up sentence that way because it invites a flood of personal opinions.) My guest, whom I'd met at Target, seemed a little overwhelmed with all the information. "It looks like one of those pyramid schemes," he responded with a confused look on his face.

I personally hate this response; it gets my gut churning every time I hear it. "Oh, a pyramid, like your job?" I quickly snapped back, thinking I was so witty with my quick quip. "That's the real pyramid, because you're an employee and you have several managers, and then they have a few managers, and then there's the CEO. You'll never be able to be CEO because you're in the true pyramid scheme!"

His upper lip tightened and he responded with the smart remark, "Why do I need to pay if this is such a good deal?"

I then lashed back with another response that led him to be even more closed off. We continued with this sword fight of words for a good ten minutes.

Did he join? Absolutely not! He left the conference room convinced that network marketing was a big scam run by a bunch of bull dogs. Had I been wiser, I could have turned his opinion around.

Maybe you struggle with "Defensive Tackler" tendencies too. If so, here are some ways to avoid this mistake.

Don't lose your cool when you hear "pyramid scheme"

I was definitely a "Defensive Tackler" when I was operating in my rookie years, and I tackled that poor young man with my harsh comebacks and never had the opportunity to tell him the truths about network marketing. When people use words like "pyramid scheme," they're giving you hints that they don't understand network marketing.

I know this because years later, when I calmed down my fiery gut to that remark, I started to ask people, "You mean illegal?" And they would often say, "No, not illegal. A pyramid, like you get this person and they get a person and you get paid." They're basically on the right path but don't know how to describe it properly.

There's no reason to become defensive, especially if people simply don't know how to sum it up with the right words. It's our job to clarify things without making them feel like they've been living in a cave for the past several decades. I may think, *Wow, you don't know what network marketing is? What rock have you been hiding under all these years?* but I now know better than to say that aloud.

Bring down the walls

Some people become closed off to network marketing because they had a bad experience with a company or had a run in with "That Guy." The best response is to ask questions and get an understanding of what happened to make them react in such a way. You'll be surprised by how much people will open up, and that will give you an opportunity to share the truth about network marketing and how it really works.

Show them how their experience can be different with you because you take your business seriously and operate with professionalism and integrity. When you come from a standpoint of asking questions to get a better understanding of their world, people will let down their walls. You'll never be able to get someone to partner with you, let alone listen to you, if you say things that make them put a wall up. When you become defensive, it triggers a response in the other person to also get defensive. Be open to hearing their experiences and really—I mean *really*—listen to them.

Action Tip: Whenever you encounter someone who has objections to network marketing, use the Feel, Felt, Found Method.[1] For example, if someone says that they don't have the time to take on anything new, respond with, "I know how you *feel*. I *felt* the same way, but then I *found* that I'm able to do this on a very part-time basis because I have a team of people who are helping me. They can help you too."

Or, if you don't truly know how they feel, mention something they can relate to. For example, if I were talking to a woman and she said, "I don't have time for this because I'm expecting my first baby in a couple of months," I (Adam) certainly wouldn't tell her, "I felt the same way." Instead, I'd tell her that my wife felt the same way.

Exercise: Have you become defensive with certain people with whom you have a close relationship? Contact them again and apologize for getting defensive. Explain that you understand that they're not interested for themselves and leave it at that. In time, as long as you operate with professionalism, they'll ask questions.

Over the years, we've found that the people who were once closed off to network marketing eventually became curious because their circumstances changed and they needed to be open to other options—or because our lifestyle changed and they finally started to see that we had a viable business.

---

1   Carnegie, Dale. *How to Win Friends and Influence People*. Rev. ed. New York: Simon and Schuster, 1981. Print.

12

The Stalker

When I think of the "Stalker," I think of the movie *The Cable Guy.* Remember the scene when Steven M. Kovacs (played by Matthew Broderick) gets home and has eleven new messages on his answering machine?

Each time he plays a message, the Cable Guy (played by Jim Carrey) says something like, "Hey, Steven, I'm at a pay phone. If you're there, pick up, pick up, pick up. Okay. I'll be home later." And then the next message is the Cable Guy saying, "I'm home. Give me a buzz. I'll be home pretty much all night." Then after several messages, he leaves a message with one of the funniest lines of the movie: "I was just blow drying my hair and thought I heard the phone ring. That ever happen to you? Anyway, call me and we will talk about it." That scene is hilarious.

Some people are very aggressive with their follow-up, maybe not to the point of true stalking, but their follow-up definitely scares off potential business partners. I remember one afternoon we hosted a blitz day where several people came over and made a large number of phone calls. A fellow consultant started following up with someone who had told him that he was interested but needed to call him back. Throughout the afternoon, I witnessed this well-meaning consultant dial that man's phone number at least seven times. I think it was safe to say that the other guy probably wanted to block his number. Fortune is in the follow-up, but there's a correct manner to do it so you don't turn off the people you need to get back in touch with.

Here are a few tips to help you avoid being the "Stalker."

Know that fortune is in the follow-up

Have you heard the statement, "No just means not right now?" It's true that nos are not forever, but that doesn't mean you should bug people every day until they file a restraining order. How much is too much? You'll get a different answer from every leader you ask. Some people stay on a leader's written list until they join or die. Some leaders make one invite and one follow-up, and are at a point in their business where they can be extremely selective.

For us, it all depends on the quality of the person. Is the person self-motivated? Influential? Professional? Someone of integrity? Coachable and resourceful? Does he or she have a track record of success? These are all factors we take into consideration when we follow up with someone. Anyone can be a diamond in the rough, but your odds of sponsoring the next rock star in network marketing go up dramatically if you look for self-motivated professionals.

Sometimes when Michelle and I are out and I get into a conversation with a server or cashier, I'll ask them if they're open to other opportunities. If they say yes, I tell them I'm expanding a business in the area and I'm looking for someone that's hungry. If they say, "I'm hungry," I say, "Great. Write down your phone number and I'll call you this week. Oh, by the way, I only call once, so if you don't pick up and I get your voicemail, call me back because I'm busy and don't have time to chase anyone. We can connect and see if what we're expanding is a good fit for you."

You might think, *Wow, that sounds proud*, but that's not the case. I'm just confident and know what I'm looking for. This technique helps me sort through people faster and save time by not following up with the wrong people.

Michelle followed up with a server one time, leaving her a voicemail message that said, "This is the last time I'll call, so if you want to learn how we can help you, call me back. If not, I wish you the best." That server called back and soon after joined our team.

Later, we asked what made her call, and she said it was Michelle's non-pressure approach and the fear of loss. She mentioned that lots of people had pitched her opportunities before, but no one ever took one away. People want what they can't have. Don't be afraid to take the business away from the wrong people or those who can't make a decision. You don't need everyone to join your business or buy your products and services.

Create urgency

Have a reason or something to share when following up with your prospect, such as a new promotion or special, a new product, an upcoming event, a conference call, or a special guest in town. Always create urgency. Don't just say, "Are you ready yet?" for every follow-up call. Most people are used to being begged into an opportunity. Professional follow-up is doing what you said you would do. You can be a pro at follow-up and not look desperate as long as you use proper posture and have a definite purpose to your call instead of just hammering them with, "Are you ready yet?"

Learn to prevent stalking

To prevent stalking, never hang up the phone or leave a meeting without setting up the next meeting/phone call. If you've been in business for any length of time, you've had prospects say, "Don't call me. I'll get back with you." In that case, I recommend getting a commitment—either a yes or a no. Tell them, "If you like what you see, great! If for some reason your not interested can you at least be bold enough to tell me no?" They'll say yes every time. Usually you'll hear, "Oh yeah, I have no problem saying no." Give them permission to be a yes or a no. Eliminate the pressure.[1]

Use voicemail appropriately

If you have a scheduled time or day to follow up with a prospect and you get voicemail, let the person know that if you don't hear back within your set time frame, you'll be calling again. If I have a set phone appointment and get voicemail, I usually tell the prospect that I'll call back in ten minutes if they don't call back sooner, just in case he or she is running late. This way the person knows I'm not giving up. It's vital that you follow through and do what you say.

If I get voicemail again, I'll let the prospect know that I'll be calling with a set time frame again. By the next day if I haven't heard back, I leave a message asking the person to call or text me so I know he or she is okay (more of a voicemail of concern, not business).

I've also learned that more and more people won't call you to say no to your opportunity, but they might text you back. If I get no response, I often text the prospect saying, *From one professional to another [I'm calling them out as a professional—that way they think, If I don't respond, I'm not a professional], can you please let me know if you're no longer interested?*

Don't be overbearing with your follow-up

We have to honor people's requests. If someone says to get back with them in a week and you call them the next day to see if they're ready, you'll upset your prospect.

---

1   Durkin, MJ. "Recommendation Selling For Your Relationship Marketing Business." Training. , . 1 Jan. 2014. Lecture.

For example, my brother-in-law recently moved and had a home security system contract he needed to fulfill. He had a sales guy he was working with to get the service transferred, but needed about two weeks to get settled before he could set an appointment for the security installer to come by his new home. Even though my brother-in-law told the guy, "I'll go with you. I just need two weeks to get settled," the sales guy called and texted him multiple times a day. My brother-in-law got so frustrated that he found another representative.

Give prospects the time they need

One of our leaders took thirteen follow-ups before he joined. I knew he would be a great partner, and he'd shown some interest, so I just kept him in the loop with different company promotions and different events. When the time was right, he joined. Remember that as you're following up, you have the opportunity to build a rapport with your prospect. Then when the timing gets better for that person, he or she will partner with you.

Action Tip: When you're trying to get a hold of someone and he or she hasn't returned any of your calls, implement sales trainer MJ Durkin's ABC voicemail system.[2] Here's an example of how it works:

"Hey Jane, it's Adam. I've left you a few messages but haven't been able to get back in touch with you. Either:

A) You're super busy;

B) You're no longer interested; or

C) I did something to offend you.

Can you please call me back and let me know if it's A, B, or C?"

---

2   Durkin, MJ. "Recommendation Selling For Your Relationship Marketing Business." Training. 1 Jan. 2014. Lecture.

Exercise: Make a list of people who have expressed interest in either being a customer or business partner when you've talked to them about your business. Determine your next company event or special promotion, and call them using this script:

"Hey Jane, it's Adam. I wanted to get back in touch with you. I know you were interested in learning more about XYZ. I just wanted to let you know of a special (or promotion) going on right now that I thought you might be interested in."

13

The Con-Vincer

Can I confess something to you? Adam and I used to be cons. Yes, that's right. I came out and said it. We used to be "Con-Vincers." We would con-vince people into joining our business. Perhaps you're now Googling us to make sure we weren't on last week's episode of *American Greed*. No, that's not the con I'm talking about. Let me paint the picture for you.

We wanted success so badly that we would tell people we would make them successful. We even had everyone hand us their lists of supposedly warm contacts, and we would call their entire list for them! It got to the point where we felt like we had a nest of baby birds all chirping away, waiting for us to hand-feed them their new consultants. At times, those baby birds would lash out and peck at us if we didn't have any new consultants to feed them. But as we took on more and more people, their lists got colder and colder. The fiasco was completely by our own wrongdoing.

Our mentor suggested that we only help people with their sharpest ten contacts, but we took it to the next level of desperate by doing all the work for them (another lesson in listening to your mentors and not reinventing the wheel). Telling people that we were responsible for their success set us up for failure because we're not that talented. For that matter, I don't think anyone is that talented! I once heard someone say, "You can drag one or you can run with a thousand."[1] We've definitely learned the truth in that.

---

1   Mason, Kim. *21 Irrefutable Laws of Leadership in Ambit Energy*. The John Maxwell Company, 2012. CD.

Here are some tips that will help you avoid being the "Con-Vincer."

Know that success in network marketing is about building leadership

The focus in network marketing is duplication. Instead of you doing all the work, it's about empowering a large group of people to do a little bit consistently that will pay off in huge amounts collectively. You can make an amazing living once duplication starts to happen in your organization. All the top earners have reached not only duplication, but also multiplication by focusing on developing other leaders within their organizations.

Empower leaders by allowing them to lead

In order to effectively empower leaders to rise up in your organization, you can't be a leader who needs to be needed. I've seen many leaders stifle their own organizations because they want to be their team's ultimate leader. They feel threatened when other people within their organization start leading their own sub-teams instead of just following them. These leaders are missing a huge opportunity for growth since they're not allowing other leaders to rise up and collaborate with them. It takes a secure leader to allow a follower to start taking the lead.

Focus on replacing yourself as quickly as possible

To prevent yourself from becoming the type of leader who needs to be needed, focus on replacing yourself as quickly as possible. Train others on your team to be able to take validation calls. Train rising leaders to be able to host conference calls, presentations, and team events. As soon as you replace yourself, start grooming another generation of leaders. Successful organizations always focus on succession. When you have a team of leaders who become stronger leaders than yourself, you can count on your organization growing without you.

Remember that you're NOT in the motivation business!

Have you ever tried to push a wet noodle? Next time you boil spaghetti, take a noodle, place it on the counter, and give it a good push. Your spouse will probably look at you with one eyebrow raised, but you'll understand when I tell you that trying to motivate the unmotivated is like pushing a wet noodle.

You may be able to say a few things that will light a fire under them for the moment, but when it comes time for them to take action, their flame will probably extinguish. Look for people who are already motivated by their vision. This business is more enjoyable when your job is just to equip and run alongside people instead of pushing dead weight from behind.

Realize that convincing people will just create more work for you

"A person convinced against their will is of the same opinion still."[2] Just because someone has signed up to be a business partner doesn't mean that he or she will actually do the work. When people join just to get you off their back, you're basically creating anchors that will hold you back from reaching true momentum. Instead, look for people who are looking for you.

My everyday motivation comes from my desire to provide a certain lifestyle for my family, and that lifestyle is all about having options and time freedom. My second motivation is knowing that there are people out there praying for a way to pay their bills or see their loved ones more. You're looking for people who are thankful for your partnership and company. Don't waste your time trying to convince others to do the work. Use the Pareto Principle, also known as the 80/20 rule, which

---

2   "Dale Carnegie." BrainyQuote.com. Xplore Inc, 2015. 28 July 2015. http://www.brainyquote.com/quotes/quotes/d/dalecarneg156636.html

states that if you focus your efforts on helping the top 20 percent of your organization, they will contribute to 80 percent of your results.

Encourage, don't close

To ensure that you and your team are taking on quality business partners, when it's time to ask for the decision, encourage them but don't close them. The difference between encouraging and closing is posture. Encouragement means that you know exactly what people want to accomplish by partnering with you, you get them emotionally enrolled in your partnership, and they willingly make the decision to get started. When you know what their personal goals are, it takes the partnership to a deeper level. Closing is keeping the partnership on a superficial level. When you close people, they partner with you reluctantly and will most likely end up doing a disappearing act.

Action Tip: The challenge for all leaders is to know exactly who to work with. How do you know the true players on your team? You can't just ask them, because everyone will tell you all the things they want to accomplish. The way to figure out your key players is to see who will take action.

We have done this with our DMO accountability groups. "DMO" stands for "daily method of operation," and anyone who deserves our time has to do three dials a day. We tell people that if they're not at least dialing three phone numbers a day, they're simply not in business. Less than three phone calls to set appointments will never get people the momentum they need to be able to grow a successful team. Calling less than three people a day is treating the business like a hobby. You'll be surprised by how many people, though they talk about their desires to become successful, aren't willing to do even the minimum to get the job done.

Exercise: Do a litmus test for your leadership. If you were to go on vacation and not take any calls for a week, would your organization grow without you? If it grows without you, then you're on the right track in developing other leaders. If not, start to empower potential leaders by delegating tasks such as validation calls, team calls, team communications, and live presentations. Start with little tasks and then give larger ones once you see that the person is reliable and competent for the task. You know you're growing other leaders when your organization can survive without you.

14

The Snake Oil Salesman

We walked in the house and were greeted with friendly smiles. The house was filled with a busy buzz as the hosts brought in tables and bowls of water. We had come to the home presentation as a favor to a friend and had no idea what we were there to see. My curiosity piqued as they started stacking boxes of a product on the table. The boxes looked strangely familiar, but it was a brand I'd never seen.

The charismatic host tore open a box and pulled out a sanitary napkin. Adam and I sat there in utter bewilderment. Suddenly, I was pulled up in front of the small group for a demonstration. She started to push on me and instructed me to put as much resistance as possible against her pushing. She then took a sanitary napkin, tore off the adhesive from the back, and stuck the sanitary napkin right on my shoulder. I was confused; that was definitely a few feet from where the napkin should go. She pushed again but this time with less force and then claimed that I had better balance because of the "miracle" sanitary napkin.

Well, I was not about to ruin her presentation, but I think we both knew her tactic. In fact, I didn't feel any stronger; if anything, I felt like an accomplice to her dupe since I just went along with her demonstration. And it didn't stop there! She advised that you could boil the napkin and drink it as a healing miracle tea. I felt like I was on an infomercial with Billy Mayes saying over and over, "But wait. There's more!"

Perhaps you've experienced something similar, or maybe you are familiar with the network marketing company that sells the magical sanitary napkins. I don't mean to poke fun. I'm sure it's a great company and product, but boy was that one of the most bizarre things I've ever had to sit through. I don't mean to chastise the presenter either. She had great stage presence, but I think it's important to steer clear from claims you can't prove.

There tends to be the temptation to over-sell a product or exaggerate income. There are a ton of great products out there that are high quality and do render results so you don't have to resort to exaggeration.

When looking to join a network marketing company, it's important to truly believe in what you're offering. If you have to be sneaky about your product and what it can deliver, it may be best to come to terms with it and find a different company to represent. Unfortunately, there are some wacky companies out there. Do your due diligence to make sure a company is reputable and has actual research backing their claims. The last thing you want is to look like a snake oil salesman or saleswoman, because that can ruin your credibility and affect your future success when you do find a great company.

Here are a few tips that will keep you from being the "Snake Oil Salesman":

Don't exaggerate income

The "Snake Oil Salesman" not only exaggerates product claims, but also exaggerates income. I have witnessed many people say how easy it is to make big money in network marketing. Big money is definitely available, but it takes hard work over a period of time to be able to make six figures and above. If a person is pitching that you can "get rich quick," you may want to rethink partnering with him or her. The right potential business partner is always truthful in how much work it will take for you to reach your desired income.

Operate with integrity

Always conduct your business like your owners—or people you would never want to disappoint—are watching. Having integrity is doing what is right even when no one is watching. It may be tempting to exaggerate just to get people to say yes, but in time, they'll find out the truth. That's no way to begin a partnership.

Exaggeration is like quicksand. Once you get into it, it's hard to get out. If you find yourself exaggerating, ask yourself this question: "Am I in this business for a quick buck or for the long term?" Trust takes time to develop but can be lost in an instant.

Action Tip: Set up boundaries for yourself so you can make the right decision when faced with temptation. Ask yourself some questions. "Do I need to hide what I am about to do?" If so, you probably shouldn't do it. "Do I need to justify my actions?" If so, don't go there. "How would I feel if the tables were turned?" If you wouldn't like it done to you, then don't do it to anyone else.

Exercise: Are there things you need to tweak in your pitch? Perhaps you only highlight the income of your #1 income earner. Instead, provide smaller incomes as well. You may be surprised to know that more people will believe you when you give them a range of incomes as an example.

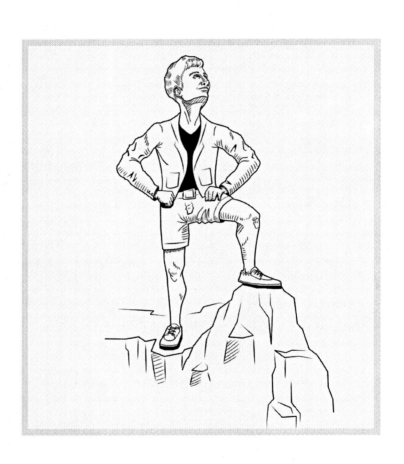

15

The Know-It-All

Odds are, if you're reading this, you're not the "Know-It-All." Reading this would imply that you don't know it all, and you wouldn't dare to pick up a book to learn something new, right? If someone gave you this book and you are a "Know-It-All," allow us to share a truth with you: You annoy everyone! Please stop! (We thought about not writing that, but there's some truth in the statement. Anyway, laugh it off.)

We've had a few run-ins with "Know-It-Alls" throughout our network marketing career. "Know-It-Alls" often shoot themselves in the foot. Let me paint a picture for you. We were having a grand opening for a new consultant, who happened to be a successful engineer who ranked high up in his company. The presentation went off without a hitch. He had a brand new consultant and two potential business partners with him.

Following the presentation, we advised him (as we do everyone) to break and answer individual questions. Since he was an intelligent and already successful person, he took it upon himself to answer questions—and also started adding things that the company needed to change!

After a long session of trying to save him from his own demise, his two potentials were no longer interested in the business and his one business partner asked to cancel his account. Lock, stock, and barrel, he shot himself in the foot, not with a pistol but with a semi-automatic weapon.

Ready for some guidelines to help you avoid being the "Know-It-All"?

Be a student of network marketing, even if you're already successful

We love working with successful professionals. They often get overlooked for network marketing because people tend to think they don't need another business. Professionals look to network marketing because they want to have more time with their loved ones while keeping up their lifestyle. Network marketing is perfect because of the ability to build passive income.

There are times when successful people come into network marketing with the belief that they can apply their knowledge in their current profession to their network marketing business. However, the results are often lackluster. Finding an already successful person who has both credibility and a teachable spirit is so powerful. These are the people who come into network marketing and have massive success regardless of being new to the business. If you're successful but have not yet done well in network marketing, that's a good indication that you need to be a student of this profession and set aside the knowledge you've gained from your current industry.

Know that even effective leaders are always students

People like to follow authentic leaders, and authentic leaders are secure enough to admit when they don't have an answer. People trust those who don't pretend to know everything. When we finally started to grow our team, I began to answer questions for potential business partners. At the time, I felt like I had to know it all. Over time I realized that we had much greater success with people when I would admit that I didn't have the answer but promised to get the answer for them. People sense when you're blowing smoke or are being truthful with your answers. They also appreciate when people don't try to be a slick salesperson and pull the wool over their eyes. Authentic leadership builds trust, and trust is the most important factor between you and the people you lead.

Realize that "Know-It-Alls" are never students

Being a constant student is crucial in network marketing, because our world is constantly changing. I recently read a statistic that "every two days we create as much information as we did from the dawn of civilization up until 2003."[1] The world is changing fast, and if we don't continue to learn, it's safe to say that we're going backward.

Personal development is crucial in this business. We see a direct correlation between the number of personal development books we've read and the growth of our income. Even during the years when we read fewer books, our income took a dip. I believe this is because leaders are also teachers. If you're only teaching what you taught yesterday, you're not effectively leading your people.

Test yourself

How do you know if you're a "Know-It-All"? Are you coachable? Are you quick to speak or quick to listen? Here's a sure-fire way to determine if you're a "Know-It-All": when someone offers coaching, do you respond with the phrase, "Yeah, but…"? You'll be surprised at how many people who ask for coaching always respond with, "Yeah, but…" When I hear those words, I can almost guarantee that they won't be able to improve their business because they're not open to learning.

---

[1] Siegler, MG, and Eric Schmidt. "Every 2 Days We Create As Much Information As We Did Up To 2003." *TechCrunch*. Blog, 4 Aug. 2010. Web. 11 July 2015.

Action Tip: Get back to the fundamentals. If you're not satisfied with your progress in your network marketing business, go back to the few action steps that result in making money. Whenever our business feels stifled, we go back to the basics and make sure we haven't overcomplicated the process.

This is crucial for seasoned network marketers because, as you grow in knowledge, there is temptation to start confounding the process. The fundamentals may be adding new customers and sponsoring new business partners. Many times, when someone starts developing a team, they stop performing those two actions. Instead, they focus on team management. As network marketing professionals, we need to focus on new growth because we will always have attrition in our business. If you focus only on management, you may one day find yourself a lone ranger.

Exercise: Create a personal development plan. The first step in growing out of "Know-It-All" ways is to admit that there's room for improvement. A personal development plan may look like this: *Read one chapter a night before bed instead of watching TV.* The goal is to complete one book per month or one book every other month. Choose books that will help you advance in your company. If you're in network marketing, books on leadership are perfect.

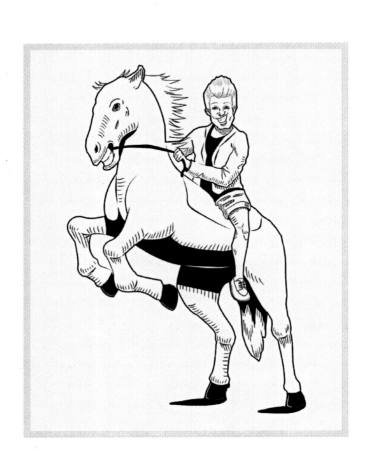

16

The Haughty on a High Horse

It makes me cringe when I see new network marketers treat others like they're beneath them because they have a regular job. They start to use terms like "J.O.B." (Just Over Broke) or call people with jobs "lemmings" (if you don't know what a lemming is, Google it and you'll probably see a picture of a group of rodent-like animals running off a cliff). While there may be some truth in those terms, they'll make people who have jobs put up a wall rather than admit, "Yeah, I guess I am broke."

I know where all this stems. We tend to want to get defensive and puff up our chests because we experience some push-back from people who don't understand our profession. In the past I also felt like retaliating after having bad conversations with ignorant people.

I remember an incident when I was a part of Toastmasters several years ago. The host of this particular chapter was a science-based company. A group of us were in an elevator heading up to a large conference room for our meeting. An older man turned to me and asked what I did for a living. I proudly told him I was in network marketing. His reply almost sent me on an internal rampage: "Oh, you're one of those."

I couldn't believe that someone would reply in such a way! I spent the rest of the day dreaming up all the snappy comebacks I could have fought back with, such as, "What do you do for a living? Oh, a scientist. Oh, one of those. How boring!" I actually came up with more awful things in my thoughts, but those are details that should never be put on paper. We must remember that "you can catch more flies with honey than with vinegar."

What I mean is that even though some of your contacts may degrade your business, you never know when life circumstances will have them wanting to inquire about it in the future. Oftentimes people say unwitting things about network marketing because they don't know the truth about it. If you suddenly alienate them, you're basically burning a bridge and digging a huge chasm between you.

Here are some tips to keep you from becoming the "Haughty on a High Horse."

Showcase yourself tastefully

Keep people wanting to know more about your network marketing business by showing them how much fun you're having at different events and how your life is improving because of your new endeavors, but avoid crossing the line into arrogance by posting demeaning things about people who have jobs. We truly have a better way, but it won't do anyone any good if you put down people who are doing what they can to feed their families.

Don't scratch with the turkeys

While you want to showcase yourself tastefully, that doesn't mean you need to suffer at the hands of those who aren't supportive and encouraging. Disconnect yourself from the mockers, because continuing to hang around them will only drain your energy and keep you from being successful.

In the beginning phases of our business, I constantly reminded myself of one of Brian Tracey's quotes: "You can't fly with the eagles if you scratch around with the turkeys."[1] A friend is someone who may not want to join your team or buy your products, but will cheer you on and refer you to people who are the right fit. That's the difference, and like I said before, many people in your life who are saying no now, will come around later.

So do things that are professionally bold to attract people. Don't cross the line and become that conceited network marketer who everyone secretly wants to knock off his or her high horse. Always remember that people may not remember what you say, but they will always remember how you made them feel.

Here is quote from Jim Rohn that you can stick in your back pocket: "You are the average of the five people you spend the most time with."[2] Along the same lines, John Kuebler also said it best when he stated, "Show me your friends and I'll show you your future."[3]

Humility is not thinking less of yourself; it's thinking of yourself less and putting others first.

In some countries and companies, people are expected to serve their leaders. However, in the world of network marketing, the best leaders serve their people. My favorite quote on servant leadership comes from Mark 10:43. Jesus states that "whoever wants to become great among you must be your servant." If you focus on serving your team rather than expecting your team to serve you, you'll never risk becoming arrogant. Servanthood and arrogance are never found in the same person.

---

1   Tracey, Brian. "Keeping Yourself Positive." Web log post. *Briantracey.com*. Brian Tracey International, 2013. Web. 28 June 2015.

2   Sato, Kai. "Why the Five People Around You Are Crucial to Your Success." Web log post. *Entreprenuer.com*. Entrepreneur Magazine, n.d. Web. 28 July 2015.

3   Gattas, Andrew "Danny", Jr. "Leadership in Today's World: Words of Wisdom from Successful Leaders." Web log post. *Hrprofessionalsmagazine.com*. HR Professionals Magazine, n.d. Web. 28 July 2015.

Action Tip: To become a servant leader, ask your key leaders two questions on a daily basis: "How can I help you?" and "Who are your key players who I should personally reach out to?"

Exercise: If you find yourself struggling with arrogance, find a way to volunteer and serve those less fortunate. There are several groups on Meetup.com that get together to serve the needy. Doing this will help change your perspective. Also, don't tell people that you volunteer your time. The motivation is different if you do it from the heart instead of for the applause of others.

17

The Basher

I was at an after-hours mixer one evening. That week there was a huge buzz about a new network marketing company that operates in our same arena. The birth of a new company often causes uncommitted people to get struck with "shiny new toy syndrome," which is when they leave their current company and jump into the new company in hopes of being one of the first through the door. There's not much wrong with that, except for the fact that those with "shiny new toy syndrome" also suffer from non-commitment and lack of focus.

Anyway, while I was there, a woman who was a fellow consultant pulled this sharply dressed man in my direction. I was thinking, *Great, another potential business connection.* She caught me off-guard when she introduced him as a consultant with the new company. I was open to talking to him—until he started bashing the company I was with, making outlandish remarks that I knew weren't true.

He proceeded to talk about how much more money I would make with them because of blah, blah, blah. I don't even remember what he said, because I tuned him out for most of our conversation. It turned out the woman who introduced us had jumped companies and was hoping he would be able to convince me to want to jump ship as well.

Here are some tips to make sure you don't become the "Basher."

Remember that we're not cannibals

Can I be bold and suggest that we, as network marketers, need to stop cannibalizing each other and bashing each other's companies? Network marketing will strengthen as a profession when we're all supportive of each others companies. All ships rise in high tide, so let's stop trying to sink each other's vessels. When a fellow network marketing company is successful, that's good news for all of us because success with one network marketing company is success in the eyes of the public—and even in the eyes of our toughest critics.

It's one thing to recruit people from another company because it wasn't the correct fit for them and they were openly searching for a new opportunity; it's another to stretch the truth to get people to jump businesses.

Remember that bashing is unattractive

There are good restaurants and there are bad restaurants. There are good churches and there are bad churches. There are good network marketing companies and there are bad network marketing companies. And here's a stone-cold fact: there are no perfect companies!

Why? Because all companies and organizations are run by imperfect people. People make mistakes, and even computers have glitches. So a perfect track record simply means the company doesn't have enough customers. Get enough customers and mistakes are inevitable. There's no greater turnoff than people who bash other companies in hopes of making their company look better to a prospective consultant. Sharing your experiences is important, but a line is crossed when the bashing starts.

Bashing happens when exaggeration meets personal opinion. Be sure that you don't cross the line and begin to morph into the infamous "Basher."

Never mistake opinion for expertise

Since the invention of Google, we've been bombarded with reviews. Most of the reviews made about any company shouldn't have much clout when people are making decisions about their financial future. With just about anything you Google, I can almost guarantee the word "scam" shows up somewhere on the first results page.

I recently listened to an Entrepreneur On Fire podcast where John Lee Dumas was interviewing Olaniyi Sobomehin. Sobomehin trains young athletes to be drafted onto professional sports teams. His business is called I'm Not You, and on this podcast he explained why he chose that name.

He shared that when he was growing up, whenever he would share his goal of being drafted into the NFL (National Football League, not the No Friends Left club), people would always come back with the statistic that less than 1 percent of football players get drafted. He would always remind himself that "I'm not you." He never considered himself to be the 99 percent; he aimed to be that 1 percent. His dream came true when he was drafted onto the New Orleans Saints.

The reason I share this with you is because you may look at the statistics and see that many people who join network marketing companies are unsuccessful. You may also find that they love to post all over the Internet the reasons why network marketing doesn't work. I promise you that the large majority of those results are not because network marketing doesn't work. If these people were truly honest, they weren't successful because they didn't work. Don't listen to the majority or consider yourself just an average person. Work hard and stay committed to becoming the 1 percent. It's worth it.

Don't company bash

Company bashing should be a red flag. Make sure you uncover the motives of "Bashers'" opinions. Is it in their best interest or yours? When professionals have negative experiences to share, they do it in a diplomatic way, whereas a "Basher" shares negative things in an aggressive and destructive way.

Be careful whose advice you take

I should include in this category the outside "Bashers" of network marketing. Have you ever had someone tell you to "go get a real job"? Don't you just love that? I've had that happen to me a few times, and one particular time I started to feel down because the person who said it was close to me.

Our mentor Esther Spina once told us, "If you wouldn't trade places with them, then don't take their advice," and that solidified with me as I sat and thought about this "Basher's" life. Sure, he was successful, but he worked more than eighty hours a week and had absolutely no time with his family. On the flip side, my mentor had complete time freedom. I also had broke friends who laughed at me, but I didn't take their advice either because I'd never wanted to trade places with them.

Remember that a title is just words

Don't mistake a leadership title for integrity. We recently had an experience where three leaders completely ruined the careers of several people because they were operating as true "Bashers." Just because someone has a leadership title doesn't mean you should follow his or her lead.

Anyway, as a result, their followers were completely blindsided. If their followers would have seen the red flags, they could have saved their future careers. All in all, don't allow greed to make decisions for you. If the highest bidder constantly gets your loyalty, you'll end up unfocused and unsuccessful.

Action Tip: If you have a question about a particular company, go to the Direct Selling Association's website (www.dsa.org) to do your research.

Exercise: If your prospect informs you they will be researching the company before making a decision here is what we suggest. Compile a list of web resources where people can make proper enquiries. Always encourage prospects who want to do research to never just Google the company name. Give them direction by providing them your list of credible sources and articles. Your prospect may still do some research outside of your list of credible sources, so you should dismantle a potential concern by letting them know what they may come across when they research online and why. Established companies most likely have some haters and competition out there that have published bad reviews. You can take that time to calmly expose the bad press and confidently stand behind your case. If you're not proactive the prospect will most likely find the negative reviews ranked high in the search engine and wonder why this information was not forth coming. This will protect them from falling prey to all the "Bashers" out there.

18

The Time Stealer

Our plane arrived and for the very first time, our feet touched land in the great state of Texas. We were beyond excited to visit our first live presentation. On the drive to the hotel, we talked excitedly about what it would be like. I imagined crowds of people in the halls anxiously waiting to get in—even people sitting on the rafters to get a glimpse of the most exciting opportunity to ever come into their lives.

Finally, the moment we had all been waiting for arrived. We opened the doors and entered the lobby, and a draft of cool air hit our faces. To our surprise, not many people were in the room and no one was waiting in the halls. We got settled in our seats and the first presenters took the stage.

One presenter in particular began to share, and as the night went on, I couldn't help but think, *My goodness, how much longer is this person going to talk?* I glanced at my watch and saw that the presentation was nearing the end of the hour. Worse, there were still two more presenters who would take the stage. A couple of people in the back quietly slipped out, and I began to devise an escape route to preserve our sanity. By the end of the night, the one-hour presentation had stretched to almost two hours, due to the "Time Stealer."

Here are some guidelines that will keep you from being the "Time Stealer."

Know that less is more

If you're a speaker for your company (presenter, trainer, or brief testimony), I speak for everyone in your audience and company when I say, "Stick to your allotted time. Don't be a stage hog!" One of my biggest pet peeves is when speakers go way over their time. When you're asked to give a thirty-second testimony, share in thirty seconds or less, not in two to five minutes. Be respectful of everyone's time, especially the guests who are attending your live presentations. When your guests are told that a presentation lasts only one hour, and ninety minutes later your closer is still closing (but is closing consultants only because your guests left), that's a problem!

Studies show that people's attention spans are very short and that the effectiveness of a message decreases the longer it takes. Many companies are now implementing presentations similar to TED Talks, where all speeches are delivered within twenty minutes (which doesn't give you the green light to give a twenty-minute testimony, by the way—twenty minutes is for the bulk of the presentation). Time yourself and please understand you are not "the show"; you're just part of it. Don't be "That Guy"!

Understand the biggest objection in network marketing

By far, the biggest objection you'll hear throughout your network marketing career is "I don't have the time. If lack of time is one of people's biggest concerns, you certainly better honor theirs and prove to them you don't need a lot of time to get your message across. If you drag out your presentation over two hours just to explain it, and they already have a full plate, I promise you no one will bite.

Whenever I open or close a live meeting or share during a home presentation, I always mention that we want to honor everyone's time and get them out within a certain time frame. People appreciate hearing that you're conscious of their time. You know they're wondering how long this meeting is going to take, so you might as well let them know to put them at ease. Just because a friend said a meeting is only one hour doesn't mean people will believe it. We've all been in situations that were projected to take one hour but dragged into two!

Remember the golden years

Always honor your word. Do you remember back when someone's spoken word was as binding as a contract? I sure don't because that was way before I was born, but I've heard about it. The first way network marketing professionals can change how people see them is to be impeccable with their word. If you say it will take five minutes, then make sure you take four minutes and fifty-eight seconds. Also, show up to appointments early, call people at the exact time you told them you would, and make sure your yes is yes and your no is no. Don't be a flake.

Action Tip: Let's talk about proper phone etiquette for a moment. People are busy, but they will often answer their phone even if they're in the middle of something. When you call, always ask, "Do you have a moment, or did I catch you at a bad time?"

I learned this from sales trainer Tammy Stanley.[1] She teaches that when you ask, "Did I catch you at a bad time?" people will psychologically say, "No, it's not a bad time. What's up?" Say this instead of asking, "Did I catch you at a good time?" because it's never a good time; you'll always be an interruption in a busy person's day.

We have tested this and it works. I always appreciate when people ask if I have a moment before they begin a long conversation. A telemarketer can call, and even when I'm busy, if they politely ask for my time, I gladly give them a minute or two. Plus, telemarketers are potential business partners, so always take their calls.

Exercise: Role-play and time the following actions so when you book these specific appointments, you'll know how much time to request:

- Phone invitation

- Home presentation

- One-on-one presentation

- Speaking portion (if you present for your company's live presentations)

---

1   Stanley, Tammy. "Carpe Phonum." Ambitious Womens Conference. , Grapevine . 1 Jan. 2012. Lecture.

19

The Prospect Thief

I'm going to step aside and let Adam tell his story here since it happened at a men's retreat he attended. I'm not sure what they did other than eat a bunch of meat and make machines that catapulted cabbage heads while grunting and pounding on their chests. So take it away, Adam!

Thank you, Michelle. Yes, we did eat a bunch of meat and we had a contest to see who could make the best catapult, but I assure you that there was no grunting or pounding of chests. Anyway, I was with a group of guys this particular afternoon. Earlier that day, I'd invited a fellow network marketer to join us. In our group, the only people in network marketing were my friend and me, and I was still building rapport with the other four.

We gorged ourselves on several pounds of meat and then got into some deep conversations (deep conversations for guys probably aren't as deep as women's conversations). My network marketing friend asked if I had shared my business with any of the others yet, and of course I said no, because I was still building rapport. The next thing I knew, he was pitching his business to them. Mind you, I'd invited him to this event and they were my contacts. He was a "Prospect Thief." I had to pull him aside and tell him to cease and desist.

Here are some guidelines that will keep you from making this mistake.

We don't need to mark our territory

In network marketing, there's an unwritten rule to never pitch the contacts of a fellow consultant or network marketing professional. Don't be "That Guy" and think that just because the other consultant has not pitched them, that it's free reign for you to have a pitch fest (if you do this, you will get "pitch slapped").

You may not have dealt with this one, but I have several times. Another name for "network marketing" is "relationship marketing," and by that definition, true professionals like to build the relationship. We are not dogs peeing on people to claim our territory, and I do believe this is a valid point.

Let's say I'm in from out of town and you invite me to go with you to your favorite restaurant. You know the owners well because you go there a few times a month. You're building rapport, and they are starting to recognize and trust you. I ask you, "Have you shown them the business yet?" and you say, "No."

How would you feel if I jumped in there and pitched the business to them that evening? Would you feel like I was in the wrong? If you said no, then you're in danger of being "That Guy." The result is, people in your company will stop inviting you to hang out. I get it, three-foot rule, talk to everyone, take no prisoners, right? But make sure you do it with integrity and respect for your fellow network marketing professionals.

It's not a shark tank

This tip should go without saying, but you'd be surprised how many people lack integrity these days. One of the biggest attractions to this business model is the ability to help a large amount of people, but that shouldn't be limited to just the people who financially benefit you. Help everyone!

Most likely, your company does business in many states or countries, so you can't afford to burn any bridges. You never know if or when you'll have a team growing in other locations. If a guest attends your local presentation and was invited by a consultant from outside the area, treat the person like your own guest. A lot of companies will talk big about the culture and the support but sometimes don't walk the walk.

Never persuade or manipulate guests by telling them they could get a lot more support if they joined your local team. If you build a business with any size, you're going to have team members in different areas and you will want your guests to be treated with that same level of professionalism. It may sound like we're in first grade again, but the Golden Rule still stands. Treat people the way you want to be treated, even when no one is looking, and operate your business like your owners are standing next to you.

If you operate with a clean conscience 100 percent of the time, you can boldly stand behind your actions and defend them with passion. When you come across someone who says, "If I join, I will do it with so-and-so," leave them alone and don't follow up. If you try to recruit them, you'll lose trust with your peers, and you may also scare away the potential customer or business partner if you do follow up.

Check your mind-set

Do you have a "lack mind-set" or an "abundance mind-set"?

Do you find yourself making these comments to others or in your head?

- "The market is saturated."

- "Everyone already knows about my service or product."

- "No one can afford my service or product."

If you do, then you have a "lack mind-set," which may make you feel desperate and possibly justify stealing a prospect or customer. Most people who commit a crime don't think they did something wrong because they justify to themselves why they did it. The "Prospect Thief" thinks similarly.

If you have an "abundance mind-set," you'll never feel the need to tear someone down in order to persuade others to join your team or company. Build your business with integrity and don't be "That Guy." Don't be the "Prospect Thief"!

Action Tip: If a prospect mentions that someone he or she knows already pitched your business, do a little research and find out if that consultant is still active before you pursue the partnership. If that person is still active, do the right thing and direct the prospect back.

Exercise: If you've ever sponsored someone who was supposed to be on someone else's team because you didn't know this unwritten rule, make a peace offering with that leader. We know that not everyone in our profession is going to hold hands and sing "Kumbaya," but righting your wrongs with other leaders is always a good move.

20

The MLM Junkie

When I close my eyes and picture the "MLM Junkie I see a lost person with the wrong mind-set and expectations of network marketing (and for some reason I see a man with a large bouffant hairstyle and a checkered oversized blazer).

Anyway, the "MLM Junkie" is someone who keeps rolling the dice, hoping that the next company is going to be the next big hit. He or she joins a company with the expectation of making tons of money virtually overnight with little effort, and then jumps from company to company, disillusioned by the myth that you can get rich quick if you recruit someone who will build your team for you or find a sponsor that will build under you.

Don't get me wrong, I have seen this happen—and I've also caught myself daydreaming about landing that heavy-hitter who brings his or her whole team from another company to ours. I think we've all dreamt about that. In reality, network marketing takes hard work, consistency, and dedication.

I'm sure you've heard the phrase, "The grass is greener on the other side." I've also heard the clever rebuttal, "The grass is greener where you water it." Network marketing has ended up with the reputation that if you don't get rich quick, then it simply doesn't work.

Please don't mistake the "MLM Junkie" for the people who have caught the network marketing bug but struggle to find the right company. These particular individuals join their first company and work hard, but unfortunately the company goes out of business. They join their next company only to be turned off by the lack of ethical leadership. They then go on a search to join the company that is right for them. They're willing to work hard; they just need to find the right fit. The "MLM Junkie" is different, simply believing that network marketing means you don't have to work hard. He or she hopes that others will do all the work.

There are several reasons not to become the "MLM Junkie." First of all, you'll lose credibility with the people you know. Picture this: Today you're shouting from the rooftops that you're representing the best company out there, but in a few months you start shouting from the rooftops that the best company is a different one. You just asked your friends and family to become your customer for one product and then you do another round of pitching when you jump to the next company. It becomes a hot mess.

Even more damaging to your credibility is representing two or more network marketing companies at the same time. So many people are a "mile wide and an inch thick." Master the success of one company, and if you want to diversify your income, add different types of businesses or investments but not another network marketing company. I find that when people do this, they become mediocre at both companies instead of great at one of them.

Another type of "MLM Junkie" is the person who had success in one company and feels entitled with every opportunity thereafter (I'm talking like twenty years afterward). If the junkie doesn't start another company with a big title, lots of cash, and tons of stage time, he or she quits and searches for one that offers royal treatment.

I totally understand that new companies need to bring in seasoned leadership right from the starting line to get the ball rolling, but what I'm talking about is different. The junkie is like the old high school quarterback who is still living in the glory days, rambling about how he used to be "the man."

I've talked to so many people who love to share how they blew up this business and blew up that business and how I'm so lucky they're considering enrolling under me. I'm still waiting for one of them to back up all that lip service. I could be wrong, but big talk is usually the kiss of death in our business.

Please don't be "That Guy" who treats the most amazing way to earn income like a lottery ticket, because it just cheapens our profession. Live your life so loud that no one needs to hear your words.

As you can see, the "MLM Junkie" fires me up. I'm getting off my soapbox now. Here are some tips so you never become one.

Do proper research before joining

Success in anything, especially building a successful network marketing business, takes focus, and it takes time to allow your team to mature. If your gut is telling you that you're not with the right company, take your time, do some research, pick one, and stick with it until you're successful, no matter what! To ensure that you are with the right company, you need to know how to do proper due diligence, and it's not by typing the company name into Google.

Have you ever Googled yourself? For some, that may be a scary thing to do. The Internet is amazing because you can find answers to virtually any question you can ask. On the other hand, the Internet can also be damaging because people can post anything they want, no holds barred.

Avoid reading opinions on sites such as Ask.com, ConsumerAffairs.com, or even Yelp. Many of these sites don't regulate complaints to ensure their truth or give the company an opportunity to defend itself without paying money. Look to sources such as the Direct Selling Association.

Any company that is part of the Direct Selling Association has gone through a strict process to make sure there is nothing inappropriate in its product claims or compensation. Other companies such as J.D. Power and Associates and the Better Business Bureau also give a more accurate picture of the companies you're investigating.

F.O.C.U.S – Follow One Course Until Successful

Once you've found the right company, remember to F.O.C.U.S – Follow One Course Until Successful.[1] Many people have asked us about the success rate in network marketing. We can confidently tell them it's 100 percent for those who never quit. You may be thinking that's a bold statement. But if others have been successful, then why can't you? If you follow what the successful people do, wouldn't it make sense to conclude that you can have success too?

I must add a caveat to this statement. You must also take action consistently. Many people quit before they even get started. They have in the back of their minds that they're just going to try it; therefore, when they experience their first bump in the road, they throw in the towel. Many people lack perseverance. They expect to become financially independent with just a few years of part-time effort. Many people will work thirty to forty years at a typical job and never reach financial independence; therefore, it baffles me when people aren't willing to invest five to seven years to achieve their financial freedom number.

---

1   Robert Kiyosaki and Donald Trump. *Why We Want You To Be Rich*. Rec. Oct. 2006. Simon & Shuster Audio, 2006. MP3.

If you want to make a living, focus on recruiting

Perhaps the reason that people jump around from company to company without making the money they want is because they're focused on the wrong actions. If you want to make part-time income, selling your product or service might do. However, if you want to make a living, you must focus on recruiting.

For some reason, people are never told that in order to have a successful network marketing career, they need to recruit other people to partner with them. Maybe it's because recruiting makes people think, *Uh-oh, pyramid alert, pyramid alert.* Since network marketers often focus on the wrong action, which is only selling their product, they make a few hundred dollars here and there. Make sure that people know the "job description" and inform them that if they want to make substantial income, they need to be prepared to recruit.

Know the difference between joining and enrolling

Did you join a company, or did you start your own business? We believe there's a difference. People join gyms and also quit them all the time. People join companies and quit them all the time too, and that's because they never get emotionally enrolled in their business. That's why, for every company that has a group of people who quit, there will always be a group of people who succeed. The difference is not in circumstance, but in mind-set.

We love listening to the Entrepreneur On Fire podcast. John Lee Dumas interviews a booming entrepreneur seven days a week. In every interview, he asks about the lowest point in his or her entrepreneurial career, and every person he interviews has a story to share.

Successful people aren't successful because they had an easy journey. They are successful because they were willing to fight for their success.

Are you willing to fight for your success, or do you find yourself always trying to take an easier route?

Know what commitment is

Our favorite definition of commitment is doing the thing you said you would do long after the feeling you said it in has left you. This is the major issue for the "MLM Junkie" because *commitment* and *loyalty* are very loose terms for him or her. I tell my team all the time that just because this is a part-time business doesn't mean that it's a part-time commitment.

Action Tip: If you are a former "MLM Junkie" and have found a company that you're committed to, still reach out to your hot and warm contacts. Ask for their forgiveness and explain your total commitment to this venture. Simply ask for their support in looking, but don't pressure them to join or buy. Most likely they will pass for now and watch to see if you truly meant what you said about your level of commitment. Once they see that you're completely committed, there's a good chance they'll partner with you or become your customer.

Exercise: Look up Eric Worre's 1-, 3-, 5-, and 7-year plan from his book *Go Pro – 7 Steps to Becoming a Network Marketing Professional* to get a good rule of thumb. In fact, if you haven't read the book, get a copy and read it. It's one of the best books for our profession. Now, write down your goals for the 1-, 3-, 5- and 7-year plans. Write out your short-term goals as well. For example, make a list of things you need to accomplish every day as well as a weekly goal and monthly goals.

21

The Networking Group Tasmanian Devil

I'm going to throw my wonderful husband under the bus here. Hey, it's okay. I've already shared all of my network marketing faux pas. Now it's time to hear about one of his (maniacal laugh).

We were pulling up to one of our first business after-hours mixers. Both of us were excited and a little nervous at the same time. We parked, and as we were walking up, we met a woman who was making her way to the restaurant's entrance. Adam, in his polite and charismatic manner, asked her what she did for a living, and after telling us, she asked him the same question. He gave his quick spiel, and when she said that she used another company, he interjected, "Well, it's time we change that," and, in a sly James Bond manner, slipped her his card.

All of this was done in less than a minute, but that was not the end. The mixer was a whirlwind of his handing out cards. Yes, Adam was once a "Networking Group Tasmanian Devil." He was exactly like that cartoon character, spinning around, saying "blah, blah, blah" with spit flying every which way, handing out his business cards left and right. Luckily for us, we learned from that evening, because when we started to approach networking with the right mind-set, networking groups became very lucrative for us.

Here's how you can avoid being the "Networking Group Tasmanian Devil."

Don't make a bad representation

We've been attending networking groups for several years, and there is always "That Guy" who tries to recruit everyone instead of giving referrals and building relationships. Yes, it's okay to want networking groups to result in more customers and more business partners, but keep in mind that the expectation of recruiting people right away will prevent everyone from wanting to do business with you or send you referrals.

Look at networking groups as a means to build relationships with potential advocates who will send people your way. The more advocates you have, the more free advertising for you and your business.

Network to build business relationships

This business is all about networking. Heck, life is all about networking. We've all heard that it's not *what* you know but *who* you know that matters. Many successful leaders have come from connections made through networking groups. Our best referrals came after a strong business relationship was formed, because people learned that they could trust us.

Let's be honest. Because of past "Networking Group Tasmanian Devils" making their way through these business groups, the most well-connected leaders often have their walls up until you prove you're not "That Guy." You can do that by being a giver. Focus on giving other people referrals to grow their businesses without the expectation of getting business in return.

Having a generous heart is attractive

Approach these groups with a selfless perspective. To be successful in networking, it has to be all about adding value to others. I hear lots of people teach the principle that "the more you give, the more you get." I cringe when I hear that statement, and you might think I'm crazy, but hear me out. I don't like to teach the "give to get" mentality (however, there is truth to the principle) because giving will have a motive attached.

Give with no strings attached, and give from a heart of generosity. Give because it's fun, and give with a cheerful heart because you want to. When you give, your needs will be taken care of, so don't worry about getting anything back. Others will see your rare selfless character and want to do business with you, and they can become lifetime referral sources. Live a lifestyle of generosity because it's the highest level of living.

Realize that trust deepens when friendships are formed

Every group has seen plenty of network marketing people come and go just looking for the quick recruit. Think about it. When people devote time to promoting their business, they most likely aren't looking for another business that day (although it does happen). Our personal success with networking groups has come from relationships that we fostered over a period of time.

I used to lead a group that was a combination of men and women business owners. We met once a week for ninety minutes to exchange leads and ideas and to offer support to one another. One of the business owners was a mountain biker, and I asked if I could go with him sometime. He was excited to have company on the trail, and we planned a ride shortly afterward.

I was immediately hooked after our first ride through the trees, over rocks, and around big dirt berms. Anytime I get excited about something, my natural tendency is to tell others and gather them to do it too. The next thing we knew, about six guys from the networking group were buying bikes and meeting every Tuesday morning for an hour ride together.

Our time together forged a deeper trust and friendship that resulted in all of them joining my team. Did I go biking just so they would join? No. I went biking because it was something I enjoyed. If not for the networking opportunities, I wouldn't have developed those relationships. Everyone has a different style. Find what works for you.

Action Tip: Attend a business after-hours mixer or a networking group. This is a good spoke in the wheel for your business, but make sure it doesn't make up the entire wheel. When it's the entire wheel, you'll feel pressured to recruit before building relationships.

Exercise: Get your thirty-second commercial perfected. When people ask, "What do you do?" be able to explain it in thirty seconds or less and always include your network marketing business. Many people who have a part-time network marketing business never include it in their thirty-second commercial. They talk only about their full-time career, which can result in a lot of missed opportunities.

Conclusion

Well, I feel like this is the end of a first date. You know, when you finally meet your dream guy or dream girl, and you have so much fun sharing experiences and insights over a nice bowl of chicken chow mein. Before you know it, the check is coming out and the server wants you to leave so he can clean up your mess and go home. I feel like that right about now, because I truly want this relationship to continue. I know Adam feels the same way, and maybe we're totally creeping you out right now.

What I mean is that we don't want this book to be our final contact with you. If you like what we had to share and you like our training style, I invite you to keep this relationship going by visiting our website: www. AdamandMichelleCarey.com. We have a free gift for you, and we aim to pump out weekly content that is entertaining and helpful for your business.

It is our hope that this book was entertaining and value packed for you. We believe that network marketing can gain the respect that it deserves if we train people to operate with professionalism. Let's work together and eliminate the stigma so "That Guy" is a character of the past. This book is an invaluable tool that can teach your team network marketing etiquette, and the best news is you'll never need to have those awkward conversations.

We also love to train about these topics. For more details about bulk orders and booking us to speak at your upcoming events, please visit our personal website: www.AdamandMichelleCarey.com.

Thank you so much, and we look forward to coming alongside you to help you create your dream life in the amazing profession of network marketing.

Notes

Sneak Attack

1   McClure, Brian. "Numbers Game, Desserts." Super Saturday. Brian McClure. North Texas Training Center , Irving. 1 June 2011. Lecture

Secret Agent

1   Jim Rohn. *Building Your Network Marketing Business*. Video Plus; 1st Edition, 2007. CD.

Lack Listener

1   John C. Maxwell, *Everyone Communicates, Few Connect: What the Most Effective People Do Differently* (Nashville: Thomas Nelson, 2010), page 3

Motor Mouth

1   Darren Hardy, *Making the Shift: Your First 7 Days* MP3.
2   Eric Worre, *Go Pro – 7 Steps to Becoming a Network Marketing Professional* (Network Marketing Pro, Inc., 2013), page 69.

Oh By the Way Phone Caller

1   Eric Worre, *Go Pro – 7 Steps to Becoming a Network Marketing Professional* (Network Marketing Pro, Inc., 2013), page 51.

2   Eric Worre, *Go Pro – 7 Steps to Becoming a Network Marketing Professional* (Network Marketing Pro, Inc., 2013), page 53.

Negative Nancy and Poor Me Paul

[1]   Maxwell, John . "." Ambition . Ambit Energy . American Airlines Center, Dallas. 1 Sept. 2012. Lecture.

[2]   Carter, Joey. "Wisdom of Mary Crowley." Super Saturday. Brian McClure. North Texas Training Center, Irving . 1 June 2011. Lecture.

[3]   *Proverbs. The Maxwell Leadership Bible.* 2nd Vers. Vol. 1. Nashville: Thomas Nelson, 1982. Print.

Nose Deaf and Disheveled

[1]   Carter, Joey. "Wisdom of Mary Crowley." Super Saturday. Brian McClure. North Texas Training Center, Irving . 1 June 2011. Lecture.

[2]   John C. Maxwell, *The 21 Irrefutable Laws of Leadership* (Nashville: Thomas Nelson, 2007), page 1

[3]   John C. Maxwell, *The 21 Irrefutable Laws of Leadership* (Nashville: Thomas Nelson, 2007), page 1

[4]   Ray Montie, "Finding Pearls," Powertrip Conference, 2014.

Defensive Tackler

[1]   Carnegie, Dale. *How to Win Friends and Influence People.* Rev. ed. New York: Simon and Schuster, 1981. Print.

Stalker

[1]   Durkin, MJ. "Recommendation Selling For Your Relationship Marketing Business." Training. , . 1 Jan. 2014. Lecture.

[2]   Durkin, MJ. "Recommendation Selling For Your Relationship Marketing Business." Training. , . 1 Jan. 2014. Lecture.

The Con-Vincer

[1.]   Mason, Kim. *21 Irrefutable Laws of Leadership in Ambit Energy.* The John Maxwell Company, 2012. CD.

[2]   "Dale Carnegie." BrainyQuote.com. Xplore Inc, 2015. 28 July 2015. http://www.brainyquote.com/quotes/quotes/d/dalecarneg156636.html

Haughty on a High Horse

[1]   Tracey, Brian. "Keeping Yourself Positive." Web log post. *Briantracey.com.* Brian Tracey International, 2013. Web. 28 June 2015.

[2]   Sato, Kai. "Why the Five People Around You Are Crucial to Your Success." Web log post. *Entreprenuer.com.* Entrepreneur Magazine, n.d. Web. 28 July 2015.

[3]   Gattas, Andrew "Danny", Jr. "Leadership in Today's World: Words of Wisdom from Successful Leaders." Web log post. *Hrprofessionalsmagazine. com.* HR Professionals Magazine, n.d. Web. 28 July 2015.

The Time Stealer

[1]   Stanley, Tammy. "Carpe Phonum." Ambitious Womens Conference. , Grapevine . 1 Jan. 2012. Lecture.

MLM Junkie

[1]   Robert Kiyosaki and Donald Trump. *Why We Want You To Be Rich.* Rec. Oct. 2006. Simon & Shuster Audio, 2006. MP3.

About the Authors

When you meet Adam and Michelle, you will instantly see that they love to have fun, but also take their calling very seriously.

"We truly believe that our calling is to be encouragers and guides in the business realm. Our passion lies in being able to speak into people's lives and see real and lasting change," says Michelle.

Network Marketing has changed their lives by giving them ownership of their time.

"Starting our network marketing business was a defining moment for us. It gave us a vehicle to be able to impact lives. Network marketing gives us a vision that the heart of the American Dream is still beating," explains Adam. "Network marketing enables us to have complete ownership of our time. We get to choose what our day looks like everyday, and much of our day is spent making memories with our daughter and family. We want that type of freedom for others, and that's what drives us everyday."

Adam and Michelle also have an online training platform that helps people who have network marketing businesses attain the same time freedom through trainings focused on Network Marketing Etiquette, Leadership Development, Personal Branding and Recruiting.

"People can have all the tools from their company work for them, but they may still struggle with getting results. We help them get better results by focusing on the personal development areas that will make them more effective," says Michelle.

Outside of their passions for business, they enjoy the outdoors and are constant students of the leaders that have blazed the trail before them.

"Reading and listening to personal development is an everyday occurrence for us. We don't consider it a task that we need to check off everyday. It's like drinking water; we feel that we need it to survive. One of our favorite books is our Bible. It has always been a guiding light for us, especially through the tough seasons of our lives," says Adam.

They enjoy spending time with their church community. Michelle shares how Jesus Culture has really impacted their vision for their business, "It's no longer about the bottom dollar, it's about focusing on the needs of people and how we can bring value to them."

For more information please visit:

www.AdamAndMichelleCarey.com